A Life of Rhyme

James C. Bennett

Copyright © 2023 James C. Bennett
All rights reserved
First Edition

PAGE PUBLISHING
Conneaut Lake, PA

First originally published by Page Publishing 2023

ISBN 979-8-88793-443-3 (pbk)
ISBN 979-8-88793-448-8 (digital)

Printed in the United States of America

Contents

Collection One: Our Journey 1
    Our Journey 3
    Our First Date 5
    Life's Worth 6
    No Bended Knee 7
    Becoming One 8
    Love of My Life 9
    Importance 10
    Hand and Glove 11
    Ireland 12
    Rescue Me 13
    A Tale 14
    No Shame 15
    Beautiful Scene 16
    Foundation of Love 17
    Bold Bond 18
    Beauty 19
    Dancing 20
    Holding You Close 21
    Ride of My Life 22
    Undying Love 23
    Little Girl Inside 24
    Support 25
    Great Times 26
    A Union 27
    Reminding 28
    Paired 29
    Spree 30
    Years 31

Our Climb	32
Inner Strength	33
Be Proud	34
Never Cold	35
Close Thoughts	36
I'll Sing	37
Collection Two: Lost Love	39
Caregiver	41
A Hidden Mind	42
Dilemma	43
Hope	44
Departure	45
Emptiness	46
Half My Life	47
Amazing Grace	48
Coping	49
The Right Words	50
Missing You	51
Flowing Tears	52
Pain and Grief	53
Living with Grief	54
Collecting Tears	55
Loneliness	56
Sounds	57
Closure	58
Lonely Path	59
Healing	60
Separation	61
Parting	62
The Wait	63
Deep Hurt	64
Isn't Sadness	65
Reconcile	66
A Better Entity	67
Regret	68
The Seasons	69

With Friends	70
Gone	71
We	72
Remembrance	73
Waking Dawns	74
Your Ship	75
Holidays	76
Intangible Worth	77
Why	78
Heavy Cost	79
Being Blue	80
Stolen	81
Making Believe	82
Castles	83
Sunflower	84
Glimpses	85
Deep Love	86
Be with Me	87
Honoring	88
Country Song	89
A Pedestal	90
Joy	91
Peace	92
A Voice	93
Different Routes	94
Caring Ways	95
Lilacs	96
Qualities	97
My Kitten	98
Carrying On	99
Watery Ways	100
Darkness	101
Philosophy	102
Collection Three: Just Me	103
Simple Memories	105
When Young	106

Childhood	107
A Dream	108
Proud	109
I Am	110
A Friend	111
A Twinkle	112
Difference	113
Truly Me	114
Feeling Words	115
Special Emotions	116
Our List	117
The Wabash	118
Your Measure	119
A Lighthouse	120
Smiling Face	121
Thoughtfulness	122
Personal	123
Complexity	124
My Lengthy Road	125
Your Tale	126
Halls of Glory	127
Mystery	128
Speaking	129
Outspoken	130
Poems	131
Numbers	132
Waters of Life	133
No Quarrel	134
Scales	135
My Story	136
Music	137
Your Quilt	138
Varying	139
Go Easy	140
Break Silence	141
Celebrating	142

    The Child 143
    Morning 144
Collection Four: Sun 145
    Sunshine 147
    Beautiful Sunrise 148
    Dawn 149
    The Morn 150
    Morning Sun 151
    And Sun 152
    Sun's Rays 153
    Shine On 154
    Sunbeams 155
    Warming Glow 156
    Spring Light 157
    Daily Path 158
    Twilight 159
    A Day 160
    Sunset 161
    Tired Sun 162
    Sundown 163
    End of Days 164
    Rest 165
    Moments 166
    Changes 167
    My Journey 168
    Brilliant Star 169
    Evening 170
Collection Five: Nature 171
    Glorious Day 173
    The Cardinal 174
    Morning Glories 175
    Forsythia 176
    Whip-Poor-Will 177
    Sky Painting 178
    Regrowth 179
    Raindrops 180

Opening Bud 181
Cycle of Life 182
Blush of a Rose 183
Full Bloom 184
Senses 185
Renewal 186
Babbling Stream 187
Wind 188
Thinking 189
Billowing Sky 190
A Picture 191
Open Mind 192
Old Man of the Mountain 193
Freshening 194
Flutter 195
Concerto 196
Wild Ferns 197
Live in the Moment 198
Birds 199
A Farmer's Life 200
Northeaster 201
Tree of Life 202
Awash 203
Be Free 204
Look Forward 205
Questions 206
Snug 207
Mother Nature 208
Kaleidoscope 209
Energy 210
Softness 211
Soft Snow 212
Jack Frost 213
Winter 214
A Drop of Rain 215
Healing Salve 216

    The Fog 217
    Wind Dance 218
    Nature's Story 219
Collection Six: Supernatural 221
    Deity 223
    His artistry 224
    He 225
    Last Verse 226
    Mysteries of Death 227
    Your Maker 228
    My Soul 229
    A Phone Call 230
    My Devil 231
    Heavenly Things 232
    Beyond 233
    My Guides 234
    Highway to Heaven 235
    True Love 236
    Let Me Float 237
    Love Song 238
    Angel's Wings 239
    Bright Star 240
    Endless Time 241
    A Gathering 242
    Valhalla 243
    Heavenly Chair 244
    Stardust 245
    Sails 246
Collection Seven: Aging 247
    Clutter 249
    Vintage 250
    Youth 251
    Don't Fear Life 252
    Earlier Years 253
    Peace Within 254
    Glitter Gone 255

  Decline 256
  Pace of Youth 257
  Weigh the Scales 258
  A Lesser Man 259
  Our Mirror 260
  Do They Care? 261
  Rewards 262
  The Temple 263
  Feeling Age 264
  Sands 265
  Recognition 266
  Over the Edge 267
  In Twilight Years 268
  Aging Gracefully 269
  Under the Skin 270
  Always There 271
  Wisps of Air 272
  A Name 273
  Child Within 274
  Blossoms 275
Collection Eight: Humor 277
  Taller 279
  Elf 280
  The Planets 281
  Piece of Mind 282
  Don't Spit 283
  Footsteps 284
  Grandfathers 285
  Baseball Game 286
  Bored 287
  What's Real 288
  A Penny 289
  Trouble 290
  Merriment 291
  Results 292
  Understanding 293

Eggs	294
Aghast	295
Being Serious	296
Aw, Coffee	297
Where Was I?	298
Forgetfulness	299
The Chips	300
Heroes	301
The Dark Side	302
Gas	303
Odors	304
Unnamed Sin	305
A Frog	306
Zero	307
Collection Nine: Imagination and Wishes	309
Imaginative Mind	311
Wishes	312
Nonexistent	313
Many Years	314
Within You	315
A Flame	316
Hang On	317
Versions	318
Hither Land	319
Your Dream	320
Clear the Reverie	321
Wildest Dreams	322
Small Things	323
Memory	324
Whispers in the Shadows	325
A Free Spirit	326
Love's Food	327
Fantasy	328
Dream	329
Father's Day	330

Collection Ten: Strength..331
    Sometimes 333
    Unique 334
    Another Look 335
    Solid Ground..336
    Life..337
    A Sturdy Limb..338
    Eroding Time 339
    Strength..340
    Eternal Hope 341
Collection Eleven: Happiness 343
    Happiness...345
    Start of Day..346
    Smile 347
    Love's Music 348
    Share 349
    Love 350
    Called Love 351
    A Kitten..352
    A Happy Place 353
    To Name a Few..354
    Slivers of Love..355
    Zipity-Do-Dah 356
    A Rush 357
Collection Twelve: Sounds..359
    Echoes 361
    Free Your Words 362
    Make a Mark 363
    Reverie..364
    Nothingness 365
    Empty Glass 366
    Shadows 367
Collection Thirteen: Life..369
    Riches...371
    Singing 372
    Two 373

    No Wrong Door 374
    Come 375
    Changing Times 376
    Tomorrow...377
    My Humble Mark 378
    Face the Day 379
    Be Thankful 380
    The Pendulum 381
    Puzzles 382
    A Blank Page 383
    Bygones 384
    Material Things 385
    A Perfect Time 386
    You Are Your Guru 387
    Greatest Place 388
    Bitterness 389
    Some Place 390
    A Woman's Love 391
    What Life Is About 392
    Own My Heart 393
    Your Time...394
Collection Fourteen: Memories 395
    Cherishing 397
    Only for You 398
    Inner You 399
    Fortunate 400
    A Cup 401
Collection Fifteen: Help 403
    Needs 405
    Not the Whole 406
    Silent Night 407
    No Bias...408
    Giving Back..409
Collection Sixteen: Paths 411
    A Toast 413
    Paths...414

A Shaft of Light	415
A Plan	416
The Candle	417
Safe Path	418
Collection Seventeen: Future	**419**
Ahead	421
Nagging Mysteries	422
What Will Be	423
Celebrate	424
Collection Eighteen: Friends	**425**
Friendships	427
Pages of My Mind	428
True Friends	429
Close Friends	430
Shed a Tear	431
Defy Time	432
Trusted Friends	433
Sing Me a Song	434
By Your Side	435
Stories	436

COLLECTION ONE

Our Journey

Our Journey

I have told in 1964
How we met.
Then came many joys
I will never forget.
There were a few
Bumps along the way.
But my love for you
Has lasted till this day.
In December of 2006,
We were dealt a terrible blow.
I print it here
For all to know.
A disease had befallen you.
This part of our journey
Did ebb and flow.
Where it would end
Was hard to know.
Our last really good
Year was 2011.
In Maine, we danced and drank
Among friends until the AM at seven.
Slowly, things began to change.
In 2014, to Costa Rica we went.
Most of the trip in a
Wheelchair you spent.
But the ocean, Piña Coladas,
And food were great.
To share our love
We did not hesitate.

Finally, January 2017,
Was a point of no return.
Not long did you have,
From the doctor we did learn.
The next five and a half months,
We journeyed together.
Like our lives, our love
Lasted through calm and weather.
Slowly, the change
From husband and wife
To a day of tears
When you lost your life.
Together we will
Always be.
But it was then
"Our journey" became history.

Our First Date

Just fifty-seven years
Exactly it was ago,
Our first date was
To a picture show.
Even though
I was discreet,
You had swept
Me off my feet.
Doctor Zhivago we saw,
But only with you
Was I in awe.
I know I'm remembering
The past,
But in my heart,
It will forever last.

Life's Worth

On my twenty-fourth
Year on earth,
You showed me
What my life was worth.
You placed your hand on my
Heart and made it beat.
The awakening of a hidden
Man—the day we did meet.
You lifted me
To towering heights.
Your sparkling eyes
Were my guiding lights.
Your smile showed
Me love every day.
Your warmth comforted
Me as we lay.

No Bended Knee

I never asked for your
Hand on bended knee.
Somehow, we just knew
It was meant to be.
Through uncovering our depths,
We revealed our soul.
It built bonds that held
Us as we grew old.
This strength of togetherness
Lifted us above the fray.
It's been more of a challenge
Since they took you away.

Becoming One

It is but a step in life
When two become one.
The walk is just beginning; they
Hope it will last until they're done.
This togetherness
Is called commitment
And bonds two
From the advent.
Many forces did strive
To test the bond's strength.
The fact that it held together
Is reflected by its length.
Smiles and love lasted
Through the years.
The walk ended and
left were only love and tears.

Love of My Life

Did I ever tell
Of the love of my life?
Ah, yes, I did, I
Know you recognize my wife.
She was so
Precious to me.
She was my life
In its entirety.
She is gone,
But her smile remains.
Locked in my heart,
I sing its refrains.

Importance

I never felt the most
Important person in life
Except when I was described
As wonderful by my wife.
It's amazing how
Your faults can be hidden
And how your imperfections
Can be overridden.
I know I've never
Been, not any day,
But I remember when she
Made me feel that way.

Hand and Glove

It has been awhile
Since I professed my love
And how we were
Partners like hand and glove.
To those who knew us,
It'll be no surprise.
They saw it often
In our eyes.
To us, our love was
Expressed in many ways.
I could write books
Describing those days.
Love does not stop
Because we're apart.
It remains forever
In my heart.

Ireland

On a hilltop,
She sat and mused.
The Irish landscape
With her was fused,
Pondering many
Castles of stone.
In her thoughts,
She was not alone.
She and I experienced
This magical land.
We brought home memories
Of walking hand in hand.

Rescue Me

Whenever I did wrong and
The Devil tried to auction my soul,
You were always there to
Buy it back and keep me whole.
If ever I'm able to float
On pearly white wings,
It will only be because
You rescued my better things.
I kept you on a pedestal,
A place where you belong.
My love was a base and
Kept us strong.
Our bonds were never
Broken through thick and thin.
How much I would give to
Live through it again.

A Tale

Come to a place
Where fantasies dwell.
You'll have an unbelievable
Tale to tell.
You're with the love
Of your life
When you just met (before) and
When she became your wife.
Only you can
Set the scene.
Make it as fantastic as
You want—it's your dream.
What a magical time
With all the frills,
Feel the love
With all its thrills.

No Shame

In my life, there
Was but one.
She even gave me
A wonderful son.
How I miss your
Presence here on earth.
I'll love you forever
For what that's worth.
If you think I feel
Shame for keeping you alive,
You don't understand
My loneliness inside.
You know the bond
We had throughout the years.
A tremendous loss,
I soothe with tears.

Beautiful Scene

There was a scene
From long ago.
A beautiful place
You and I did go.
As if painted for
Us to see,
We stood absorbed
In the ecstasy;
And by nature,
I was kissed.
Your beauty was also
High on my list.

Foundation of Love

Love, an all-encompassing word
When used to describe
A union of years.
The strength of two
Who shared
Both joy and tears.
A foundation built
With pillars for each
To lean upon,
So solid that happiness
Exists forever beyond.

Bold Bond

You sat by me
And held my hand.
Our love blossomed;
That we did understand.
We knew not what
The future would hold,
But we knew together
We could face it bold.
For many years,
This bond did exist,
And our tribulations
We did dismiss.
It is hard to do
As well-being just one,
But I'll do my best
Till the setting sun.

Beauty

Simple beauty can be
Captured by the eyes.
This beauty sprang forth
As if overnight to my surprise.
They were planted by
Loving and caring hands.
For years, they've bloomed
Without any demands.
It seems our pleasures
Of life we can retain
To remind me of her beauty
Again and again.

Dancing

We danced until it was
Impossible to dance anymore,
Loving it though we weren't
The best couple on the floor.
To us, just flowing to
The music was a special treat.
Now I close my eyes and
Have a memory of my moving feet.
I can still feel her
So gentle in my arms.
Making me feel wonderful
Was just one of her charms.

Holding You Close

I held you close
After we met.
I held you close when
Children we did get.
I held you close
For many years.
I held you close
Through smiles and tears.
I held you close
When you were cold.
I held you close
As we grew old.
I'm holding you close
Though we're apart.
Yes, I held you close
When we met.
Now, I'm holding you close
So I'll never forget.

Ride of My Life

How was I to know
I was in the ride of my life?
And how was I to know
You'd become my wife?
It awakened my emotions,
That day we met.
And not for one second
Do I have any regret.
As blossoms open up
In the spring,
What wonders into
My life you did bring.
You stirred a heart
That lay dormant for years.
Like riding a roller coaster,
We had no fears.
My glass stands empty,
But I've filled it with tears.
Here's to you, my love.
Thank you for fifty-two wonderful years.

Undying Love

I was in love with you
Before we met
And what a stimulating
Feeling the day we met.
Then for years, no greater
Love could we get.
Even though we've parted,
I've my undying love yet.
It is a forever love
That I won't forget.

Little Girl Inside

She never lost
That little girl inside,
Whether it be skydiving,
On a motorcycle, or a horseback ride.
I'm not sure where she
Got such a love for life,
I only know she made
My life complete as my wife.
Somehow, she knew what
To do that made people smile.
She never kept hers hidden,
It shined all the while.
Even when her
Future looked dim,
A simple I love you from
Her gave strength to Jim.

Support

Sometimes, you need somebody
To hold your hand
And to listen carefully
And understand.
Your problems, they
Are willing to share.
What great support
They're just being there.
You can see love
Shining from their eyes.
Clearly, they care for you,
This you realize.
How great it was to have
Had someone like that.
What a special person
This woman named Pat.

(Patti)

Great Times

I think, most
Often than not,
What treasured memories
I have got.
Five decades and
Two years plus
Were the greatest
Times given to us.
Sometimes, it was
A roller-coaster ride,
But we always
Had our love by our side.
We always had our
Boat set neat and trim
And sailed through
Life with troubles slim.

A Union

A long time ago,
Enjoined as one,
Inseparable, this union
Had become.
Our world expanded
With family and friends,
But nothing came between us,
Together till the end.
Through joys and tears
This oneness persevered,
Sharing many memorable years.

Reminding

Did the snow fall gently
For you on certain days?
And did the moon reflect silvery beams
Off the snow to show your varied ways?
Was the warmth of lights within houses
Put there to remind me of your love?
Now I lay on the softness of my pillow
To remind me of your tender touch from above.
Were music and laughter created to
Remind me of your enchanting smile?
Precious, you were brought into
My life and gave it meaning for a while.
Now everything I see, hear, or feel
Exemplifies that you're still there
Because you are my love forever, and
Each day reminds me of what we did share.

Paired

Forever above
My only
True love.
Closeness we shared.
How did we ever
Get paired?
You—so special.
Me—a swain.
Our chance meeting,
Something did ordain.
It's said
Opposites attract;
Our union must
Have been a fact
That was written
In a higher almanac.

Spree

What a beautiful spree
This trip as one.
How precious the
Memories have become.
And as if this union
Of minds and souls
Were blessed and
Through eternity holds.
We are forever together
Even though apart.
The souls can't be separated,
They became joined from the start.

Years

The years we loved each
Other and spent as one
Seemed to fly by, but
We lived from sun to sun.
The sun has set for
Your journey through time,
But you'll always have
A special place in my mind.
Someday, through
Time, our belief and space,
We'll sit, hold hands,
And kiss and embrace.

Our Climb

Our climb was never
Too steep along the way,
Even though it may have
Been difficult on a particular day.
With caring hands we helped
Each other rise above it all,
We cradled the other so as
To prevent any terrible fall.
Since that glorious time that
I was given in my life,
Each step is now a struggle
Without my loving wife.

Inner Strength

She lived as long as
She did because she never grew up.
I'm not speaking of height,
I mean how life filled her cup.
When the burdens of giving birth
And raising the kids were gone,
It was as if the little girl
Within began to sing her song.
From skydiving, riding horses, the
Ocean, and driving a school bus,
Each adventure she met
Head-on without any fuss.
Loving her with all my
Heart also kept me young.
When she left, she took a part of me
With her; now it's memories I'm among.

Be Proud

Where have they gone,
The days of old?
They shouldn't be forgotten,
I am told.
You can't bring them back
Or relive them again,
But be proud of the fact:
Many battles you did win.
The first twenty-four you
Fought on your own.
The next fifty-two
You weren't alone.
Then came two
That left you blue.
The days of old—gone.
Look to the new.

Never Cold

As the time passed,
Our lives together
Stayed very bold.
How did we cling together?
Our love never grew cold.
Through your smile,
Our story was told.
How special you were.
You made our lives solid gold.
Now you live in memories
That will never get old.

Close Thoughts

I've written a
Quip or two,
And memories I've
Shared a few.
I've written of the one
Who was my true love.
As you know, she now
Dwells in a house up above.
There is no way for
Words to tell it all,
But we loved till the end
When the angels did call.
Now thoughts hold
Her close to me.
Here I'll save her
This place for eternity.

I'll Sing

I'll sing your praises
Till I can sing no more.
It'll be with a loud voice
Till I reach the other shore.
Let all know how you
Lived your life,
How you supported this man
For years as his wife.
You now dwell in
A land of peace.
You surely have ascended
To say the least.

COLLECTION TWO

Lost Love

Caregiver

The toughest job I ever
Had was primary caregiver.
Each day, no matter how you
Felt, you had to deliver.
Someone depended on you
To ease their pain
And make their life safe,
Whether sunshine or rain,
But I would do it
A thousand times more
If you were still here.
I'd gladly accept the chore.
Seeing your eyes open
Each passing day,
Gave me strength to face
Come what may.
When it came time
From this job I was fired,
It left only half a man,
His services no longer required.

A Hidden Mind

You were always in there.
Of that there was no doubt,
But some days it was hard
To find your way out.
Other days, with help
From above,
You made it out,
And we could share our love.

Dilemma

I sat by your bed
On the tenth of June,
Counting your breaths,
Knowing your life would end soon.
My hand on you assuring
Me life was still there,
Hoping on hope that you
Knew I did care.
My thoughts ranged from
Love to release.
I needed you to stay
But wanted you at peace.
You were being called
Away from me,
But telling you that you could go,
Left me with guilt and misery.
Just know I loved
You that day.
You leaving has left
A void along the way.
I will never lose you
In my heart and mind,
Such is the strength of our
Love, it will forever bind.
But now I must let you
Be at peace and content.
Part of your soul in my heart,
I've shared all that we've meant.

Hope

My mind has
Become clear.
I remember
The year
The doctors gave
Up on you to mend.
I never would
Come to that end.
So for five months,
I kept our hope alive.
From a sometimes adult
To child and baby did you arrive,
We were together
To the end.
It was hard, but it was
The last time we had to spend.

Departure

On June tenth, I began
My path alone instead.
Sadly, I stood by
The side of your bed.
This was the last time
I'd watch you lay your head.
Your fight was long,
And you fought it well.
Quietly and on angel's wings, you
Ascended with the ringing of the bell.
I know where you were welcomed
Based on the life you led.
But I hated to see you go
As I stood by your bed.

Emptiness

Peace and love can
Be singular things.
You may have had love
And all it brings,
But when love's gone,
It's hard to release.
No matter how you try,
There is never peace.
It's like staring into
An empty pit.
You can't bring love
Back, not even bit by bit,
But it will always be
Hidden in your depths
Because it was so great
As a memory your mind accepts.

Half My Life

June tenth is
A solemn day.
It is the day
You passed away.
You seemed at peace
When your time came,
But it was sad
All the same.
Half my life
Went slipping by.
I can't forget
Even if I try.

Amazing Grace

With pipes, violin, and
Bagpipe, they played "Amazing Grace."
My head in hand, I wiped
The tears from my face.
The emptiness welled
Up from within.
To miss someone so sadly
And know not where to begin.
When you were nothing
And given the greatest gift of all.
Then only to watch
Your castles fall.
Your strengths and forces
Are drained from you.
What is a
Poor wretch to do?

Coping

I am but
A simple man,
Trying to cope with life
As best he can.
I stand as one,
My pillar gone,
But I will face
Life all alone.
I aspire not for
Wealth or fame,
Only to be with one
Who I gave my name.
A smile, a word of
Love, a tender touch,
If again these could
Be, I would give much.

The Right Words

I have searched for days
For words to share.
I am having a very hard time,
Finding ones without her here.
There are words that would
Comfort others but only bring me pain.
They speak of a time when my
Life sparkled and was free of rain.
I will mention a few that I've
Lost along with your smile:
Love, peace, togetherness,
Hope, and comfort. It's been awhile.

Missing You

Have I ever said
How much I miss you?
Have you ever seen tears
In my eyes of blue?
Can you see
How I ache?
Do you know you going
Away caused my heart to break?
Can you feel the love
I still have for you?
I hope you can;
I know others do.

Flowing Tears

If you've stood alone
For many years
And there are days when you're
Filled with nothing but tears,
You wonder where has that smile gone
And those squinty eyes.
Are they lost somewhere
In past blue skies?
If there's an empty space
In your arms and heart,
You realize it's been that
Way since you're apart.
Then a precious
Vision comes into view,
And the emptiness becomes
Sated as your love comes to you.

Pain and Grief

Without a doubt, the best of my
World was taken from me.
Will there be no bright tomorrows
For me to see?
I have shared my
Grief and pain,
But it can never
Bring back that love again.
I guess I should feel
lucky I had it at all.
This woman who made
Me feel proud and tall.
I know if she could,
She would tell me to cease
Being so morbid
At the very least.
But I can't stop carrying
Forth the torch, love, and tears.
It will stay with me
Even if it takes years.

Living with Grief

Grief is a
Never-ending path,
Experiencing a loss that
Splits you in half.
It may stay hidden
For days and days
But will make surprise
Appearances—it has its ways.
The most insignificant
Moment, place, or things
Can bring it forth and
Tug on your heartstrings.
Grief keeps on coming;
It just won't quit.
To survive, you somehow
Learn to live with it.

Collecting Tears

If, for some reason,
You shed a tear today,
You know why, but
You don't have to say.
I have a collection
That I save in a vial.
They have accumulated
For a long emotional while.
I'm saving them
To cleanse my face
So it will be bright and
Shiny when reunited in your place.

Loneliness

Loneliness is a burden
That you bear alone.
To some, it's like
A weighty stone.
The heaviness of silence
Can pierce the bone,
But recalling memories
Can bring you back home.
Love is unbreakable especially
Remembering that smile you have shone.

Sounds

Why do we weep because
Of words or sounds?
What causes our heart
To ache with no one around?
Is it imagination when
We see you in a dream?
Is our emptiness
As much as it seems?
It's not fantasy that
You still exist.
I go to sleep and
Know I've been kissed.
One of these sounds
That I have found
Is Willie Nelson's "Angel
Flying Too Close to the Ground."

Closure

Why is having complete
Closure so hard to do?
Is it because of the strength
Of love taken away from you?
Didn't you cry enough or
Experience enough pain?
Why do you have to live
The parting over and over again?
I think it may be a way
Of keeping them forever near
Even though half of you was
Ripped away amidst many a tear.

Lonely Path

As I continue through
My path of life,
I do so without
My loving wife.
I admit that
Sometimes, it's a lonely one,
But hope and memories
Bring a morning sun.
A new day brings on
A challenge anew.
I only need the
Company of few.

Healing

When your tears flow
Freely in a heartbeat,
No control have you
To stay steady on your feet,
So give in to emotions
And don't regret.
The love within you
Is for them yet.
Only time will heal
This awful pain,
But even then,
Grief will remain,
So don't even try
To close this door.
You can't because
You'll love them forevermore.

Separation

This feeling for you
I won't let go,
A deep love many people
Will never know.
I feel sad for others
Who have not known this bliss.
They cherish a
Feeling, a touch, or a kiss.
As one, separation was
Our greatest fear.
Here we are now for
More than a year.
You've gone your way
To peace and repose.
How many years before
Being together? Who knows?

Parting

If you've stood beside
Someone for years,
When they're gone,
It brings on tears.
Then when all
The tears are shed,
You're only left with
Memories instead.
Yes, your life
Is incomplete,
But cherished thoughts
Are so sweet.
Remembering the love
Helps you back on your feet.

The Wait

I'm alone now,
But who does care?
Think happy thoughts,
Not despair.
The years we had
Together were so great.
They overcame all
And cleared the slate.
Together, we were
A tower of strength.
Separated, I
Can only wait.
How I love you
Only I can know.
Your love for me
Will always show.
I close this out
For all to see
That all we had
Was ecstasy.

Deep Hurt

I guess there are many
Ways to mend an ailing heart,
But we all know there is
No way to fix one torn apart.
Nothing anyone can say
Can touch this hurt.
It will remain with you
Until you return to dirt.
This week they may
Fix the beat,
But the pain I feel will
Stay till again we meet.

Isn't Sadness

It isn't sadness,
Thinking of her laugh.
It isn't sadness,
Remembering her smile.
It wasn't sadness, watching
Her give the babies a bath.
It isn't sadness, dwelling
On the past for a while.
If I completely lost
What isn't sadness,
I would only
Be half a man,
So I'll remember what
Isn't sadness while I can.

Reconcile

Quietly, your path was ending
As I lay beside you.
Begrudgingly, I accepted that.
You had lived all you could do.
Gladly, I would have gone for
You or with you all the way,
But your journey was yours to
Take while I had to stay.
I can have my fantasy that
I can feel your hand in mine
And become drowned in the pools
Of your eyes; Yes, I'll be fine.

A Better Entity

Do you know how much you took
Away when you left?
But there will always be a
Special place for you at rest.
Always within me,
You will stay and beyond.
Someone as special as you
Must live on.
Your eyes, smile, and touches
Built confidence in me.
Your moods and feelings
Were a challenge, you'll agree.
Greatest of all, your love
Made me a better and stronger entity.

Regret

How many times did I pass you
By without giving you a hug?
How many times did I feel it
But didn't say these words of love?
I can't bring back those
Moments, this I regret,
But not grasping those
Chances, I can't forget.
Forgive me for these
Opportunities I missed
And for the times
You should have been kissed.

The Seasons

You are my spring;
You bring rebirth
To us all.
You brighten
The summer
And glean peace
In the fall.
We say goodbye in winter
With all that it brought.
Your life was awesome,
How hard you fought.

With Friends

You are up there,
Can you see?
Tonight, it's just
Black Velvet, Willie, and me.
What did we miss?
Where is that kiss?
You are always
My most precious thing.
The poets of
Such things sing.

Gone

You flew away
On golden wings,
Never to again touch
Earthly things,
But your beauty
Pleasant memories bring.
The sun, smell of flowers,
And birds that sing
Cannot surpass
Just your being.

We

For some reason, I felt
You with me today.
That you are at peace,
This I do pray.
This is no special day
To bring a memory to me,
But nonetheless,
You became my We!
I need these
Moments of bliss.
I cherish this time
And give you a kiss.

Remembrance

I remember you in the morning light.
I remember you when the sun is bright.
I remember you especially at night.
You always made my world right.
I will always remember you.

Waking Dawns

How many mornings
Have we greeted the day?
Did we do it with
Loved ones as we lay?
Those were the most
Precious days of all.
Also, the lonely ones
I now recall.
But remember every
Waking dawn,
The ones with true loves
I cherish now they're gone.

Your Ship

There is a time when you
Must walk your path alone.
Do not count on others
To increase your comfort zone.
You have seen that many of
Your friends and family have gone away.
Your destiny happened to be to stay.
But your years have prepared
You for the trip.
So muster all your strength and wits
And become captain of your ship.

Holidays

As the holidays
Grow close,
My heart aches
for you most.
I'll miss your love
This time of year.
You brought out love
For all with abundant cheer.
You were my most
Precious gift of all.
No greater gift
Can I recall.
So be with me in
Mind and soul.
My love for you
Will not grow cold.

Intangible Worth

I find myself
With possessions aplenty.
My need is not for
Material things of many.
My lack is of
What I've had inside.
I cherished it and
Flaunted it with pride.
If ever an angel
Came to earth
To teach me
What life was worth,
It was my love
Gone passed.
But she was my pillar
And gave me love that will last.

Why

Why is it that birds
No longer sing?
Why is it that bells
No longer ring?
Why is it that my
Eyes no longer glisten?
Why is my heart heavy
For the one I'm missing?
You might also be
Asking why
When the love of
Your life has gone by.

Heavy Cost

As I sit tonight with
The glistening of my eyes,
My heart has grown
To twice its size.
I, again, am feeling
It is you I've lost,
And being alone is
A heavy cost.
But I will always
Feel your soul.
It puts together a broken
Me, making me whole.
All I need to do
Is see your smile.
It brings your love
Back to me for a while.

Being Blue

I heard a voice speak
Softly to me tonight.
It asked why was I
Blue? Was I all right?
I know the answers
She already knew.
It was time for
A holiday or two.
To live these days
Without her here
Are without her
Love, joy, and cheer.
What carries me to be
With family and friends
Are memories of our
Love that never ends.

Stolen

A thief comes not
Only in the night.
He steals in daylight,
Hours while out of sight.
He steals those emotions
That you try to conceal,
Of loved ones who have passed,
The pain he will reveal.
Though years may pass,
The grief does not.
He will make tears flow,
Not a few but a lot.

Making Believe

I'm making believe
You never left me.
For a time, I hold those
Memories from getting free.
It is not hard to close
My eyes and drink my fill
Of all the nectar
The flowers of love did spill.
I dance to love songs alone,
Feeling you in my arms.
As if floating on air,
I feel all your charms.
If you think those
Are tears I shed,
It's just clearing a place
For you in my head.

Castles

Many castles were
Built of stone.
Mine is not as you've seen
By the images I've shown.
Some things seem
To last forever,
I thought so when
We were together.
But castles and homes
Will come and go.
My love for you will
Always be, this I know.

Sunflower

The sunflower is
A regal flower.
When I see it now,
I feel your power,
How you loved
This sturdy bloom.
There are images of it
In every room.
Its beauty brought
On your glorious smile.
So in every room,
They'll stay for a while.

Glimpses

I glimpse you beside me
In the shadows of the world.
I see your beauty
When the clouds come unfurled.
I feel your love in dreams
Where in your arms, I'm curled.

I miss you.

Deep Love

Speak of love
And call a name.
Deep rooted memories
Still remain.
Although our lives
Won't be the same,
Forgetting a loved one
Would be a shame.
Keep the love close,
Touching your soul.
Remembering good times
Never grows old.

Be with Me

When at peace,
My words do flow.
They tell of times
When pleasures we did know.
If I am ever to wake
From this reverie,
I hope that you
Are with me.
In a trance or
With a mind clear,
I want you
To be forever near.
Hold my hand,
Guide me on future paths
That will find me
With you at last.

Honoring

You are special.
In reverence, do I speak.
Honoring your memory
With heart sad and weak.
Keeping you alive
Daily in my mind.
You were so lovely,
Beautiful, and kind.
You have your wings
And soar on high.
You were taken from me,
And I can't reason why.

Country Song

When I hear a
Country song,
Sometimes, I
Sing along.
Some songs put
Me in a trance
With memories of how
We used to dance.
I miss holding
You close.
Just being with you,
I miss the most.
There is no justice
It seems.
All we could be doing
Together are just dreams.

A Pedestal

How can we conquer
A troubled mind?
Remembering one
Who was so kind.
A smile that would
Truly capture your heart.
It possesses you
Even when being apart.
I speak to you often
On bended knee,
Hoping on hope
You will hear my plea.
On a pedestal,
We've placed you for now,
Knowing we'll be
Together someday somehow.

Joy

I can feel the joy
You bring to me,
Captured in the memories
Only I can see.
Others have their memories
They hold within.
But only those between
Just you and me was I given.
These are special to me
This time of year.
They bring me peace and warmth;
They are so dear.
I smile and laugh
Because they keep you near.

Peace

As I sit alone, I wonder
How long it's been
Since I've felt a tender touch
By a loved one and remembered when.
Still I feel the affects
Of that warm embrace
Even though it's not
Happening face to face.
As sure as you'll always
Be my shining star,
I will seek comfort from
Knowing you're not far.
A gift I was given
So long ago.
I'm thankful to have had it;
I still feel the glow.
Curtains of dusk
And tingles of soft sounds
Bring peace to me,
Knowing your love still abounds.

A Voice

Your voice echoes
In a cloud.
It comes to me
Very loud.
It speaks of the pleasures
We have known.
It tells me
I am not alone.
So clearly can I
Hear it say.
There is nothing
You need to repay.
The union we had
No one could break.
I'm always with you,
Make no mistake.

Different Routes

We are asked to
Accept all things,
To believe that
There is good in all life brings.
Excuse me if I
Have my doubts.
I'm sure that life
Could have taken different routes.
I have lost a lot
In many a day.
Was I that bad
That I should pay?
Is there no mercy
For us left behind?
My view of life is
That it's cruel, not kind.

Caring Ways

From ashes to ashes
And dust to dust,
I loved that you did,
But you shouldn't have fussed.
You made me feel so
Special with your caring ways.
I tried to repay a little
During your needy days.
For all our days
From when we met,
Your place in my heart
Is still there yet.

Lilacs

Just another year and I see
The lilacs bloom without you.
You loved the fragrance, and
Into the house you'd bring a few.
The odor sparks memories of
How they made you smile.
As long as they bloom,
They bring you to me for a while.

Qualities

When you pass on and
Remain in the heart of another,
You do not die, but
You live on forever.
Those qualities that were
So special about you
Remain within those
Loved ones who knew.
The simple things
Will they cherish.
You will live forever;
You will not perish.

My Kitten

Today is one of
Those emotional lows.
How my heart aches,
And it shows.
No longer was it
Meant to be.
This page of history,
It's been torn from me.
But life can not erase
What was written.
I love you still,
My precious kitten.

Carrying On

Four years ago today,
A big part of my world was gone.
I was at a loss, wondering
How I would carry on.
For days, weeks, months, and
Even years I would stumble and fall.
I wept, shed tears,
And out loud, I would bawl.
Grief bursts were often,
Remembering it all.
But life goes on, and
I, with happiness, recall
The good times and love
That was not small.
This picture of you
Keeps you alive.
You gave it to me for my
Birthday when I turned twenty-five.

Watery Ways

What are tears
But liquid love,
A way of expressing
Thoughts from above.
They come with pain or joy
In your cheeks or eyes.
They're a way of
Making us realize
How we feel or felt
About someone true
And shed at times
When happy or blue.
There have been many days
In the past few years that I've
Expressed my love in these watery ways.

Darkness

Lost in the darkness
Of a lonely night.
I was rescued and given
Hope by my guiding light.
How was I blessed
With an angel on earth?
Did I really deserve
To hear what I was worth?
Do we ever know how
Our path will be lit?
Being lifted out of darkness
Saved me, I must admit.

Philosophy

I spoke to myself when
Alone the other day.
I know not to ask questions
Because I know what I'd say.
But sometimes, I need to
Discuss some philosophy,
And there wasn't another
Person there but me.
So I asked myself, *How many
Emotions will create tears?*
My answer was, *Many that
You have experienced through the years.*
*Can you elaborate and
Name a few?*
*The strongest are love and hate
To name just two.*
*I know you cry at times,
What makes it so?*
*A special part of my life
Was called to go.
Now missing that part
Surfaces with strong emotions,
Bringing tears to my eyes
That would fill the oceans.*

COLLECTION THREE

Just Me

Simple Memories

Did you ever ride
In a rumble seat?
Did you ever squish mud
Through the toes of your feet?
Did you ever get leeches
While wading in a pond?
Did you ever share a sundae
With two straws with someone fond?
Did you ever wear a
Penny in your shoe?
Did you ever hold a
Kitten that was brand new?
Did you ever ride
On a running board?
Did you ever play a
Stick that was a sword?
Did you ever hang a bathing
Suit on a car mirror to dry?
Did you ever shoot off
Bottle rockets on the fourth of July?
Did you ever use a cardboard
Box as a sled?
Did you ever keep a
Flower that was dead?
If all of the
Above you have done,
Then you've lived many
Years under the sun.

When Young

It's been so long
I hardly remember when
I lived on a dirt road
And played with a friend.
Our playthings were sticks
That were our swords and guns,
Skipping stones on the water
To see how far it runs.
Our forts were built
With many a limb.
He's gone, but I still
Remember him.
Our world was the
Woods and a pond.
Each day, we expanded
Our world on and on.

Childhood

Our indoor entertainment was
Listening to *The Shadow* on the radio.
For the rest of our
Fun, outside we would go.
Catching frogs, turtles, and
Salamanders busied our hand.
Sometimes, we would play
Kick the can
Or toss rocks to see
How far they would land.

A Dream

I dreamt of when
I once was young.
It was about a time
When songs were sung.
Your feet hardly
Touched the ground.
There was mirth and
Happiness all around.
Not a care did
You hold for long.
You were invincible,
Oh, how strong.
Then I woke amidst
My glee
And saw the person
I've come to be.
I saw a man
Who was weak and frail,
But he could tell
You one hell of a tale.

Proud

I weathered the
Snow and the rain.
I withstood heat
And cold again and again.
I admit the years
Have taken their toll,
But I've never
Been on the dole.
I did whatever
I needed to do
To pull my children
And family through.
I stood up and
Answer to no man.
Yes, I am still able
And do what I can.

I Am

He has stood before
Many a man
Without his hat
In his hand.
He had no reason to
Beg them to forgive.
He did his own thing,
And his life did live.
His actions were never
Intended to harm.
For people who loved him,
It was just his charm.
If you saw it different,
A different point of view.
Number yourself mistaken
And among the few.

A Friend

People may ask
Of what you are proud.
Stand up straight
And answer aloud.
Only if you did me
Wrong and lost my trust,
Did I ever find cause
To give you a fuss.
I never went to
Look for a fight.
But when I had to,
It was given all my might.
Forever a friend,
I will stand by your side.
If not, it's a boot
As I give you a ride.

A Twinkle

When you see a twinkle
In his eye,
You may stop
And wonder why.
But friends who've known
Me for a while,
Realize it's
Only the child
Trying to get out
And tell the world
It's all about the
Humor of life unfurled.

Difference

Is there only
One true you?
Is there anyone
Who really knew?
Ask one hundred people
To describe this man.
One hundred answers you may get,
Being different on demand.
Because as our lives changed,
We also mutated and grew.
Only to view our whole life
Can anyone know the true you.

Truly Me

I never lived my life
With style and grace,
But if I had something to say,
I'd say it to your face.
I know on occasion,
I've offended a few;
But where I was coming from,
They certainly knew.
With relationships, I tried
To be honest and true.
Color my heart red
And my intentions true blue.

Feeling Words

Artists paint pictures
Of all kinds.
I try painting pictures
In the mind.
Artists put down
What they see.
I try to put down
What I feel inside of me.
Artists can step
Back and view.
If you feel what I said,
That will have to do.

Special Emotions

Kittens, puppies, and babies
Bring out the best in me.
Special emotions are
Created for these, you see.
Certain things in life
Go way beyond
All the fishes
In the pond.

Our List

Thoughts welled up
From deep tonight.
I felt to share
Them was only right.
It dealt with
All the things I've done.
I'm actually
Proud of some.
Others I wouldn't
Care to name.
I only have
Myself to blame.
Let's look on
Ourselves with forgiveness
And hope our wrongs
Are the shortest list.

The Wabash

This person I have
Come to be
Will not be remembered
In pages of history.
He was not a tyrant
Or a national hero.
He wasn't like George
Washington or Nero.
He lived a simple
But joyous life,
With four children
And a loving wife.
He will leave this world,
Atoning for his wrong,
Singing the "Wabash Cannonball,"
His favorite song.

Your Measure

A word, a thought, or a sight
Is all that you need
To create beauty that
Is inside you indeed.
It flushes forth
And rolls off your tongue,
Spewing things like love,
Desires, and memories unsung.
You need not dig deep
To find these pleasures.
Be yourself and honest,
This is what the world measures.

A Lighthouse

Climb the spiral staircase
To the light on top.
Turn it on to warn
The ships to stop.
Now they can avoid
The rocks of doom,
And give them wide berth
With ample room.
Come to my cove
With safe harbor within.
There my face will shine
As I greet you with a grin.

Smiling Face

If you're up
Or if you're down,
Bring on a smile
Or a frown.
So always keep a happy
Thought in reserve
To bring forth the smile
That others deserve.
They like to see
Your smiling face.
It's like giving them
A warm embrace.

Thoughtfulness

When asked if I'm a
Thoughtful man, I rarely will reply.
If you don't know the
Answer, I don't know why.
If you've known me
For a long, long while,
You'll know that being
Thoughtful is part of my style.
If we've just met and
A friendship needs to grow,
Just ask those who have
Known me, they'll tell you so.

Personal

Some people choose their
Subjects not to offend.
Mine will be personal,
Getting myself to mend.
There's a strange humor
In this old man.
He has a duel with
Life as best he can.
I have a home with
Warmth and food to eat.
Outside can be cold
And stormy and chill my feet.
I need not many
Pleasures to make my day.
My complex mind
Helps along the way.

Complexity

When you're asked your favorite
Number, color, or zodiac sign
So some guru or seer can
Cubbyhole you and your life defined.
If you believe this
Can be done,
You put a lot of faith
In an opinion of just one.
You are complex,
And you are who you are.
You're not a five or red or because
You were born under a certain star.
If you think you know me
And plot me on a chart,
You have another think
Coming, that's a good place to start.

My Lengthy Road

I haven't needed much
As I've strode along.
A true love and an
Occasional Willie Nelson song.
A sip of nectar
To make life sweet,
Someone to share
My every heartbeat.
I've had these
Greatest gifts bestowed.
They have helped me
Along this lengthy road.

Your Tale

I have had but
One tale to tell,
And I hope that
I've told it well.
Make the most of
The here and now.
Include as much love
As your time will allow.
Build memories that
Will last forever.
Make a bond for an
Eternity with him or her.

Halls of Glory

Walk in the
Halls of glory.
Let everyone
Know your story.
Shout it from
The highest peaks.
Put your name on the
Lips of them who speaks.
Even if it's
Only in your dream,
Your life is more than
What it might seem.

Mystery

If you don't want
The unforeseen, don't follow me.
Only those needing mystery,
Trailing in my footsteps, should you be.
We aren't promised a
Primrose path.
If you can stand a little
Grief or an occasional laugh,
I welcome you by my side
To travel beyond.
Maybe together, peace
Can be found.

Speaking

Silence has never been
A strong suit of mine.
Most times, I speak
What's on my mind.
Sometimes, it's
With tongue in cheek.
Other times, to make a
Point I seek.
My thoughts take the
Form of all kinds.
Read carefully, some
Lurk between the lines.

Outspoken

It's said you should make
Ripples but not waves.
I guess it refers to
The way one behaves.
Being outspoken or
Holding your tongue
Changes as you grow older
Than when you were young.
Some of us only
Knew one way.
We never couched
What we had to say.
You either liked it
Or it raised your ire.
What other explanation
Do you require?

Poems

My pen has been
Silent for a spell.
Not many poems written
But I've had stories to tell.
The tales are to paper
And may see their day.
I don't care if they're liked,
It's what I had to say.
They were high
On my bucket list.
An accomplishment for me,
If you get my gist.

Numbers

A mathematician,
I am not.
But take one from two,
I know what you've got.
You have a number
That stands alone,
But it still has
Strength of its own.
It can be more powerful
With a times or a plus.
This adds to life
And becomes a better us.

Waters of Life

The waters of life
Have washed for years,
Taking away our layers
Or so it appears.
Does it show
What lies beneath
Once we have shed
Our protective sheath?
Is there a warm body
Or a cold heart?
Is our smile sweet
Or is it tart?
We stand on the pile
Of layers, are we bold?
Or is our greatest
Story yet to be told?

No Quarrel

Many a stone
I have thrown.
Defiance
I have shown.
Now I dwell on
What has been
And have no quarrel
With my fellow men.
A life that was full
With its ups and downs
Brings on smiles as
Well as frowns.
I am who I am,
And I love life and friends.
Will you accept me as I am?
That's all that depends.

Scales

During our past, our halo,
On occasion, has slipped.
But the scales of justice,
We hope we have not tipped.
And when our accounts are tallied
And all is said and done,
We pray to be with loved ones
Forever after our setting sun.

My Story

If ever my
Story is told,
Will it be weak
Or will it be bold?
Will it tell of
A man with true heart?
Or will it speak of a
Soul cruel and dark?
It may vary depending
On whom you ask.
There are those who love.
Others may take me to task.
But if you've been true
To me and done me no harm,
We have walked through life
With love arm in arm.
Fault me if you will,
This I can't alter;
But look at yourself,
Was it you who did falter?

Music

To me, there is nothing
More powerful than a country tune.
They can make you happy or cry
Or fly you to the moon.
Powerful tunes like "and I
Will always love you."
Or a tune that captures a
Feeling when you are blue.
Who cannot relate to a loved
One who has wings that abound
Especially when they play
"Angel Flying Too Close to the Ground."
Or who cannot feel the pleasure
Of dancing with your wife
When they play "could I have
This dance for the rest of my life."
Or when Willie causes
Your heart pain
With his recording of
"Blue Eyes Crying in the Rain."
Or an enchanting song
That engulfs me.
Nothing says it like
The "Unchained Melody.'

Your Quilt

Like a stream, life does
Not move in a straight line.
It bobs and weaves,
Creating no route defined.
See it as an ocean
That ebbs and flows,
The precious tides in your life
Weave a quilt that shows.
And like the waters
On this earth,
What is left in life
Shows your worth.

Varying

If you were asked to describe
A person in just one word,
You might be surprised by the
Various answers that you heard.
But you need to realize a person
Is not the same to everyone.
A person possesses emotions
On the surface and deep down.
Therefore, the person chooses
Who sees what and when,
Different even for
Those loved or
Accepted as a friend.

Go Easy

Sometimes, in the
Search for peace,
Step back, relax,
Let your chances increase.
It might reveal for you
What was there all along.
You were moving too fast and
Missing the lyrics of the song.
The melody and the words
Will make you content.
You just have to feel
What the vibrations meant.

Break Silence

How strong the
Sound of stillness becomes.
It pounds in your head,
Penetrating your eardrums.
It has a rhythm
All its own,
A steady beat
When you're all alone,
Then pierce the silence
With a word or two,
Just knowing the world
Will always renew.

Celebrating

If you did not
Celebrate with me
When alive,
Do not mourn for me
When I'm under six or five.
I may not recognize you, do you see?
So your presence
May mean nothing, do you agree?

The Child

Sun shining bright this
Morning through the window pane.
Contrary to popular belief,
I'm really not insane.
I know you may not believe
It based on some things I've done.
But it was just my way of
Enjoying life and having fun.
The twinkle in my eyes
And the impish grin
Only tells of the child who's
Trying to escape from within.

Morning

Opened my eyes,
Then out of bed.
To the kitchen,
My footsteps led.
Finally, with a cup
Of coffee in my hand,
The morning was eagerly
Waiting my command.
What reward today
Will be my prize?
I've already been given
One: I was able to rise.

COLLECTION FOUR

Sun

Sunshine

"You Are My Sunshine,"
Was but a song,
Although it spoke of
Wanting you with me all along,
Making me happy
While shining on me,
Staying with me
For an eternity.
I still love hearing
This refrain today
And wishing it true. "Don't
Take my sunshine away."

Beautiful Sunrise

I saw life this morning;
It captured my eyes,
A simple thing,
A beautiful sunrise.
Deep into my soul,
It was so bold
To reveal strong emotions
From days of old.
How precious
These memories
That surfaced today.
It showed me a path;
I'm on my way.

Dawn

What light I see
O'er yonder hill.
Comes to me
With air so still.
Feel the freshness
Of the dawn.
A new adventure,
Bring it on.
Even with a
Morning dew,
I'm happy to wish
A good morning to you.

The Morn

As night flows into morning
And we bid the dark adieu,
What pleasures await us or
Can we create for me and you?
You knew just how to please
Me with your touches and your smile.
I'll greet the sun each day,
Knowing we'll be together in a while.

Morning Sun

I really love
The morning sun.
It's an omen that
The day can be fun.
Its warming rays
Go deep within,
Telling old bones
To let life begin.
It clears black clouds
That cover me,
Saying, "Step into today.
Let history be history…"

And Sun

When the sun shines,
It has a limit.
Like life,
You live within it.
But if the sun
Was all we knew,
Romancing at night
Would have come to few.
Don't wish for something
That won't come true.
Hold to the pleasures,
They'll see you through.

Sun's Rays

Do not linger on
Glimpses of the past.
Embrace tomorrow
When the sun's rays
Are again cast.
Feel life around you
From all you see.
Put things behind you
As a cherished reverie.
Your path should
Lead far ahead,
And only in your memory,
Should exist where it led.

Shine On

Shine bright, oh,
Glorious sun.
Spread your rays
Till the day is done.
Let your warmth
Make my spirits soar.
Unsatisfied, I will
Want for more.
You have brought joy to
My life in days gone passed.
Keep on shining
And make it last.

Sunbeams

Sunshine beaming
Through the rain
On this
First of May—again.
In the distance,
Colors are forming an arc,
Making this a
Glorious day to embark.
A giddy feeling,
Buds galore.
Lift your spirits,
Let them soar.

Warming Glow

As the sun
Sifted through a cloud,
This glowing orb seemed
To speak aloud.
It told of
Things gone past.
It told me of
A love that last.
It spoke of its
Warming glow.
I think it just
Wanted me to know
That rising for the
World to see
Opened up a
Universe of mystery.

Spring Light

What yonder light
Do I perceive?
A gift of life
We all receive.
It says, "Smile
And face the day.
Clear your mind
And look my way.
Feel the warmth
Of what I bring."
Yes, I feel you,
Come on, spring.

Daily Path

Where is the sun
When it goes down?
Shining on another land
It can be found.
If we wait awhile,
It will come to us again.
We can smile and say, "Hey,
Old Sol, where have you been?"
Then he will wander
Across the sky,
Making shadows all day long
Before again it is goodbye.
Does he get tired
Of this daily pace?
I can only compare this to
The way we seem to race.

Twilight

Twilight speaks softly
As it welcomes the night.
It glows, recalling
Today, all was all right.
It knows it must fade
And leave light behind,
But it also knows the joys you
reaped will stay in your mind.
So sleep tight, my friend,
And welcome the sun anew.
Then hope for another
Twilight that is kind to you.

A Day

When evening draws near,
The curtain of night falls,
But we still feel the warmth
And bask in it all.
As ever when day ends,
It's always with pleasure.
We still have our friends.
Be thankful and treasure.

Sunset

Whenever the sun
Begins to set,
Remember the love
You used to get.
It was as if
It would last forever;
It lifted you up in
Stormy weather.
It will never
Leave you behind.
In your memories,
It will always be kind.
The break of day
And setting sun
Is how long our
Love will run.

Tired Sun

As the sun was setting,
It let out a sigh,
"I'm tired from a long day.
I'll just sink into the sky."
Who knows what
Tomorrow will bring.
Today gave a hint
Of the coming of spring.
A day of remembrance
Of a day long ago
When the future was destined,
This we know.

Sundown

With the sun going down
And twilight near,
Put a smile on your face,
Belay your fear.
Your life will be measured
By what you've done.
Remember the love,
Kindness, and fun.
There have been some wrongs
But none too bad.
Helping put warmth in some
Hearts should make you glad.

End of Days

Thank you for giving
Me these years of gold.
Please be kind to me
As I grow old.
While I can,
I'll sign a pact.
I'll try to enjoy
But not foolishly act.
I can't promise there
Won't be a quirk or two.
If there are, let it
Bring smiles to a few.
And when my
Merriment is done,
Let me slip into calm
Waters toward the setting sun.

Rest

As the sun
Begins to set,
I feel close
To you yet.
A warming glow,
It will share,
Running its last fingers of
Light through your hair,
As if your
Spirit floats free
To seek a higher
Destiny.
Knowing there
Is comfort ahead,
Lay down and rest
Your tired head.

Moments

A beautiful sunset
And I reminisce
The time sitting together
When we shared a kiss,
Snuggled in arms
That spoke of our love.
We cherished the moments
Like on the wings of a dove.
And yes, I recall
You were by far
The most beautiful of all.

Changes

The sun bids us
A pleasant night,
But dark clouds
Threaten rain it might.
Would you care
If you were hunkered down?
Because tomorrow, maybe
It'll just be the sun around.

My Journey

Many a day I've seen
The sun arc crossed the sky.
I've marveled as the moon
Changed shape as the months went by.
Saplings have grown from three
Feet to many yards tall.
My journey has been joyous
And hard, but I've survived it all,
Sitting here counting the
Stars sparkling above,
Knowing the greatest gift of all
Was being given my one true love.

Brilliant Star

Look at the
Brightest star above.
Does it point to
The one I love?
Or does it show
Me where to go forth?
I know to get there,
I must go North.
What awaits me
If I travel far?
Will I still be
Chasing this brilliant star?
Or will my journey
Be a place of rest?
To find the answer,
I'll continue my quest.

Evening

The stratus clouds this evening
Refracted the setting sun's light.
There were pinks, reds, oranges,
And purples to fill me with delight.
What a magnificent colorful
And mind-capturing display
That nature has given us
To end this day.
It makes you wish this
Scene forever you could keep
And with you each night,
Giving you peaceful, restful sleep.

COLLECTION FIVE

Nature

Glorious Day

Hello, morning,
Don't be sad.
Stop your crying,
All is not bad.
Put a smile
On your face,
Warm up to the task.
Be a glorious day,
Is that too much to ask?

The Cardinal

A cardinal landed on
My window sill.
"Please give me some
Seed if you will."
"I certainly will
If you'll sing me a song."
It sang its heart out,
Melodious and long.
Seed aplenty
It did get.
Its beautiful song
I can't forget.

Morning Glories

Fingers of light
Crept over me,
Putting my
Thoughts to flight.
What pleasures it
Exposed for me to see?
On cue, the morning glories
Opened much to my delight.
The smell and beauty
Lay bare my inner glee,
Freed my mind to open wide
And absorb this marvelous sight.

Forsythia

My poor forsythia
Is terribly confused.
Much so that it
Has me amused.
It wants to keep its
Green leaves
But changes some
To purple as it please.
Then not knowing what
Season it really is,
Puts yellow flowers in
Bloom to show it lives.

Whip-Poor-Will

How I love to hear
The whip-poor-will
As he sings a tune,
On old Clay Hill.
He greets the evening
With his song,
Hoping a mate
Will come along.
I never tire of
His refrain.
I wait each evening
To hear it again.

Sky Painting

Things pass
Before your eyes
Like a beautiful
Painting in the skies,
Framed just for
Your delight,
Such a calming,
Soothing sight.
How soft it is
In the fading light.
It brings you peace
For the oncoming night.

Regrowth

Sipping some wine
And enjoying the rain,
Knowing it will bring on new
Growth, all will be green again.
Soon flowers will grow,
And all the birds will sing,
Which brings on new
Hope of a glorious spring.
If you can't be with people,
Enjoy what you have.
It will help with what
Hurts like a healing salve.

Raindrops

I watch as raindrops are
Delivering messages from above.
Can't you feel how
They are transporting love?
They choose what is
Individually for you.
Their pure, cool drops
Wash away a few
Teardrops and sorrow
And give you life anew.
As they cleanse and write
New words on the slate,
It brings a fresh new
Look of love on this date.

Opening Bud

Come, little bud,
Burst open to the world.
Share your pleasure.
Let your beauty be unfurled
Like a babe emerging
From the womb.
It is a challenge as
Before you, life does loom.
We await your arrival.
Your praise we'll sing.
We're tired of winter;
We really want spring.

Cycle of Life

Today, from the kitchen
Window, I watched leaves fall,
Another cycle of a life
Sorrowfully not for all.
Those gone before me
Is quite a large list.
What we all shared
Is surely missed.
They paid their dues,
And left their mark.
Some, only a whimper;
Others, a loud bark.

Blush of a Rose

The blush of a rose
Captures the poet in me.
It speaks of love
And tranquility.
Its fragrance
Fills an empty space.
Its beauty is like
A warm embrace.
It brings forth
Another beauty from within
That has lived on and on,
Since we did begin.

Full Bloom

Open, morning glory,
And spread your glow.
Let the sun realize
That you know
How to greet a
Day in full bloom
And share your beauty
To erase all gloom.
You look so frail
With your pastel hues,
But it's your boldness
The morning doesn't lose.

Senses

What contrast
Nature does create,
Displaying her beauty
There is no debate.
Colors soft and soothing
To ease the mind,
Awakening your senses,
Inner thoughts to find.
If this doesn't put
A smile on your face,
You don't belong in
The human race.

Renewal

I love this color
That greeted me at dawn.
It is so refreshing
Without white on the lawn.
I admit there is beauty
In white as well as green.
But now, renewal of life
Is everywhere to be seen.
The warming of the days
Dwells in your heart as well,
Lifting your emotions
As if by a magical spell.

Babbling Stream

When emotions flow
Like a babbling stream,
A healing release
It does mean.
For it cleanses
The wounds unseen
And creates room
For a pleasant dream.

Wind

The wind is blowing
Strong today.
Hopefully, it will bring
All the good our way.
See the trees wiggle
As if dancing to a tune.
Feel the sun's warmth
Dream of what's coming soon.
Even without the green,
It is a beautiful day.
Snuggle in a blanket
Of white and enjoy your stay.

Thinking

This morning, crisp and
Cool—felt like fall.
No woodchuck, rabbits, or
Squirrels, where were they all?
They were probably snug
and warm in their home
As am I with no desire
To get out and roam.
These old bones are content
To sip on coffee and rest.
Dreaming of days gone passed
Is what I do best.

Billowing Sky

When you sit
'Neath a billowing sky,
You can muse
And wonder why,
But answers aren't
Sometimes easy to see.
They can be buried
Deep within you and me.
Soaking up the sun,
And enjoying a warm breeze
May help and be needed
To put your mind at ease.
Your troubles can become heavy
And weigh you down.
Be at peace with yourself.
Lift your spirits and erase a frown.

A Picture

As if looking out a window,
The world is yours to see.
Has it been framed with all
Its wonders just for you and me?
We know it was created
With beauty both soft and crisp.
A baby, a sunrise, or lush green
Kissed by the morning mist.
The grandeur of the Rockies
Or the wind sweeping over the plains.
The picture of a loved one
Captured in your heart and remains.
We all have our private window
Into which we can peer.
So make it what fills your soul with
Something you can always hold dear.

Open Mind

Nature paints in
Many forms.
A frame of ice
Yet your eyes it warms.
If you only
Feel the cold within,
Open up your heart and
Let the beauty flow in.

Old Man of the Mountain

The mightiest of mountains will
Crumble and be carried to the sea.
You are also strong, so
Don't dwell on your frailty.
Even the Old Man of the Mountain
In New Hampshire didn't last,
But many pictures taken of
Its grandeur preserve its past.
Your strengths and your beauty
Will be remembered as well.
Maybe in photos or in
The stories people tell.

Freshening

Everything looks so much
Greener after an April shower.
You can feel a
Freshening hour by hour.
There is a new life
Given for us to see.
It creates emotions,
And makes you feel free.
How can you not
Look out and smile?
Let your spirits soar and
Be happy for a while.

Flutter

Flutter your wings,
Beautiful butterfly.
Let me feel free like
You and soar in the sky.
Your colors and patterns
Are catchy to my eye.
A lost love you could
Be, I don't deny.
If you were
Sent to me, I wonder why,
But I may never know
Until I die.

Concerto

A time to let
Your mind escape.
Lying close to a stream,
In it, let your hand drape.
Feel the coolness, let
It soothe your nerves.
Feel the warmth of the sun and relax.
It's what your body deserves.
You close your eyes and hear
A gentle breeze,
Creating a concerto
Among the trees.
You can imagine a loved
One there to share.
For in this reverie,
They can be with you anywhere.

Wild Ferns

Come to where
The wild ferns grow.
A place only you
And your true love know.
Let it embrace you
In comforting arms.
Feel all of
The pixie charms.
Laugh and be
Filled with glee.
Smile at the beauty
Meant for you to see.
Come let it put your
Mind at rest,
And remember days
That were the best.

Live in the Moment

I miss the flowers
And hearing birds sing,
All those things
That spring will bring.
As the days grow longer,
Then it will be May.
Before you know it,
Farmers bring in hay.
But the sun is shining
This very day.
Live life and smile,
Don't wish it away.

Birds

Bright and brisk,
This morning was.
The birdfeeder
Was all abuzz:
Blue jays, cardinals,
Nuthatches, and chickadees.
Colors and songs for
My eyes and ears to please.
A woodpecker worked
On a wooden post.
These are some of
The things I like most.

A Farmer's Life

The meadowlark sang,
And the pigeons cooed.
The chickens were fed,
And the horses were shoed.
The cows were milked
And the pigs slopped.
Even cleaned the barn
Where the cows had flopped.
He put grease on
The wheels of the wagon.
It's not quite noon,
And his butt's drag in.
They say a woman's
Work is never done,
But try a farmer's
If you want some fun.

Northeaster

If you feel a northeaster
Coming your way,
It's in your cabin
You should stay.
Just don't forget
To trim the sails,
Grab a bucket, you
Might have to bail.
Batten all the hatches
On the boat
And hope the old
Crate stays afloat.

Tree of Life

The tree of life
Has spread her boughs
To protect him
More than life allows.
She has sheltered him
From sun and rain,
Given him her shade
And relieved his pain.
Only when her
Branches fall,
Will he have
Lived it all.
Then his time
Will see leaves shed,
A time when he and
The tree are dead.

Awash

Water droplets fall
To the ground.
We see them, but
They don't make a sound.
How soft they feel
On my skin,
Creating sensations I
Can feel within.
As with life, they
Won't last forever,
But I'll enjoy them
As long as they give me pleasure.

Be Free

As you stand in
A cathedral of trees
And you feel a
Cool, uplifting breeze,
You know this is a
Place of song,
A place where even you
Can do no wrong.
Let your heart and
Soul be free.
The world is
Yours to see.

Look Forward

March snows, and April showers
Have come in May.
Spring flowers—jonquils, lilacs buds—
Are here to stay.
Sunshine, swimming, and
Picnics are on their way.
Look forward, friends, better
Days are coming. Be happy and gay.

Questions

See the feathery
Clouds in the sky.
A wisp of air
And you wonder why.
Fragrant, soft earth
On which you tread,
Do you wonder
When instead?
Questions are what
Are given to man,
But is it for
Him to understand?
Or should he just
Enjoy the ride?
Keeping loved ones
And memories deep inside.

Snug

Beautiful snow but
Still cold and raw outside.
Just me and Willie
And Southern comfort snuggled inside.
These are times when
The house speaks to me.
I feel you in every corner,
On every wall—your memories here to see.
They say only a drunk
Drinks alone,
But I know
I'm not alone.

Mother Nature

Mother nature's very beautiful
In her gown of white.
She says, "It won't be long
Till the sun is bright.
I may change
Dresses in between.
But by March seventeenth, I'll
Be wearing green."

Kaleidoscope

I found myself
Staring off into space,
Then I became aware
Of a beautiful place.
As if time stood still,
It was held for me to see,
Expanding its horizon,
Setting my mind free.
It allowed me
To create a kaleidoscope,
Bringing forth brilliant
Colors filled with hope.
Let me keep
This pleasant view
Until I can
Share it with you.

Energy

Flashes of light
And a rumbling in the sky
Filled with vibrant
Energy for you and I.
Feel the tingle on
The hairs of your neck.
The sights and sounds
At your nerves do peck.
This wonderous sight
Is ours to love,
A tremendous display
Of strength from above.

Softness

As the rain falls
Gently all around,
It is removing much
Snow from the ground.
If you let it wash
Away your gloom,
I'm sure brighter
Skies will bring bloom.
Its softness is like
A soothing touch,
Bringing with it
Happiness, contentment, and such.

Soft Snow

A soft snow
In April falls
To the brook.
It will widen its walls.
Soon it will make
The flowers grow.
Love will be in the air.
Warm winds see the water flow
Like blowing hair.
I love you
And know you're still there.

Jack Frost

I stepped outside this
Morning to greet the day.
Jack Frost chimed in saying, "If you're
Wise, in your house you'll stay."
With icicles on my whiskers,
I beat a hasty retreat.
I had to hurry because
I feared frostbite on my feet,
But the sun was shining,
And its warmth felt kind.
With this glorious orb rising,
Could spring be far behind?

Winter

Winter is a stubborn season;
It doesn't want to go away.
This morning, at zero degrees
And forty the other day.
I know spring doesn't
Have far to come.
I noticed buds on the
Lilacs, encouraging to some.
I look forward
To the warmth ahead.
Only one of the reasons
To get out of bed.

A Drop of Rain

A drop of rain fell
Into my life today.
It asked me, "Do
You mind if I stay?"
"No, be my guest.
Welcome to my home.
I hope you don't mind. I've
Brothers and sisters. I'm not alone."
Bring them all; I look
Forward to what you bring.
I know you'll make the
Flowers bloom for me this spring.

Healing Salve

A gray sky because
The clouds hang low.
Contrasted by the black
Of trees and white of snow.
This morning, Mother Nature
Has not much color to show,
But brighter days with
More warmth are coming, we know.
Just enjoy your life
And savor what we have.
Smile and live,
It's like a healing salve.

The Fog

When your path
Is obscured by fog,
Grab a photograph to
Give your memory a jog.
Or if someone kept a
Journal, all the better.
You can relive the
Path to the letter.
Some things we certainly
Need help to recall,
But there is a huge amount
Of pleasure remembering it all.

Wind Dance

How beautiful and happy the trees
Look dancing with the wind.
I could feel the rhythm
Surfacing from within.
I can't hear the melody,
Much less do I know the verse,
But swaying with gentle motions,
There was no need to rehearse.
As I stepped forth, the trees
Began to whisper to me,
"Come, join our dance
And let your emotions run free."

Nature's Story

A flash of light,
And a distant rumble
Make you feel
Weak and even humble.
Then there's the rising
And setting of the sun
Whose magnificence and
Beauty can't be overdone.
Feel a soft rain
And a lilac smell.
Ride on a moonbeam,
A love story to tell.

COLLECTION SIX

Supernatural

Deity

At what point on
The scale of time
Did man's consciousness
Begin to climb?
Where he thought
Beyond only him,
To wonder what
Was over the rim.
What happened after we
Became a lifeless form?
Were there calm skies
Or a forever storm?
Was there more than
Just an end?
If so, who could
Have made it and when?
It would have been
Someone greater than he.
Then he pondered calling
It a deity.
He liked the fact of
Something beyond.
So he believed in a god
Of whom he became fond.

His artistry

When we've been given
A beautiful morn,
It is out of his artistry
That it's been born.
None of the masters
Can match his feat.
They know it's impossible
To even compete.
You feel loved that
You've been given this view.
With his brush, he
Can capture every hue.

He

It's said the oceans
Are where life did start.
Putting chemicals together
Was very smart.
At some point, the chemicals
Began to replicate.
We don't have
A given date.
Pleased was he with
What was done.
Then he toyed with
Combinations just for fun.
Eventually, he put
Life on land.
Some believe his mistake
Was when he created man.

Last Verse

When the angels are
Singing your last verse,
Join right in,
No time to rehearse.
Sing it proudly
For all to hear.
If slightly out of tune,
Don't have any fear.
Friends and loved ones
Really won't mind.
They'll cherish your legacy
That you're leaving behind.

Mysteries of Death

What will it be
Like when I'm done?
Will there be darkness
Or will there be sun?
Will I look the
Same as when I die
Or will I look like I did
When I was young and spry?
Will we be vapor or will
We be tangible things?
There are many mysteries
That death brings.
Will we be joined
With the departed anew?
Will there be many
Or only a few?
What will we need
To sustain our soul?
Will we exist as a part
Or will we be whole?
Will my true love be
There to welcome me home?
Or will I stand by
Myself all alone?

Your Maker

The greatest church I know
Is in a cathedral of pines,
Wading in a brook or on top
Of a mountain—it takes all kinds.
When men of various cultures
Began to organize their god,
They lost track of the fact
That we are all in the same pod.
Whatever you call your maker,
He wants only good.
Love, kindness, helping, and
Sharing should be understood.
Wars have been fought trying
To preserve one name.
The supreme being is the supreme
Being, the name's all the same.

My Soul

I stopped and looked
Into my soul
And found some things
That were bold.
There were mysteries
Hidden deep inside:
Love, hate,
Compassion, and pride.
Some were dealt to me
On better days
And go back
Quite aways.
Others I brought
To bear.
Some, I'm ashamed
To share.
I hope I'm forgiven
By someone above.
Erase the demons,
Leave only the love.

A Phone Call

A phone call to heaven
Would be so nice.
I'd gladly go in debt
And pay the price.
Being a toll call,
The time given would be short,
But we could affirm our love
With words of support.
Just to hear her voice
Other than in my mind
Would be so wonderful
And so unbelievably kind.

My Devil

If I ever truly
Let my devil loose,
Beware, dear hearts,
He's a loony goose.
You should run for
Cover or at least duck
And don't get mired
Down in tons of muck.
You should keep your
Back to the wall,
And into his mirth, be
Careful not to fall.
He will show you
Much fun along the way,
But you should know the
Terrible price you must pay.

Heavenly Things

She wove golden
Threads year after year,
No heart was bigger
Or so dear.
She had a smile
You can't forget.
I can hear her
Tender words yet.
She will take her
Place among heavenly things,
Being with the angels
And wearing her wings.

Beyond

My life has voids,
But I exist.
All my best friends separated
Or vanished in the mist.
The togetherness is
What I miss,
A friendly hug or
A loving kiss.
There are many versions
Of what lies beyond.
There is one for which
I am fond.
That is that
Reunited we will be
To cherish what was dear
For eternity.

My Guides

How many friends have
I had along the way?
Some, passed in a whisper; others,
Like the breaking of a glorious day.
I am counting on them to be
My guides when my time is done.
Take my hand and lead me
To a land with a radiant sun.
I know they can attest to
The fact my heart was true,
And stand beside me
In a world joyful and new.

Highway to Heaven

The highway to heaven
Has been a difficult climb.
Many stumbling blocks have
Tempted my fun-loving mind.
The path has seen
Detours along the way.
The pleasures of life
Sometimes caused me to stray.
If it had been easy, would
You think it worth the trip?
But you've washed away the
Obstacles drip by drip.

True Love

What is lurking
In the shadows of my mind?
Is it a precious memory
Left for me to find?
Maybe there's a halo
Given as a guiding light,
Trying to clear the way
To bring things clear into sight.
I know I see a beautiful
Face smiling back at me.
Then I know it's my
True love here for eternity.

Let Me Float

Come be with
Me awhile
And I'll be
Captured by your smile.
Lift my spirits
To float upon your wing.
Caress my cheek
As I hear the angels sing.
I know more than a second
Is too much to ask,
But give me that second
If it's not a great task.

Love Song

Sing me a
Song of love.
Send it to
My angel up above.
Let it tell her
I still care.
Remembering the
Love we share.
You live in my
Mind and heart
Even though
We're apart.

Angel's Wings

Our memories are floated
On angel's wings,
Carried aloft which
Causes your heart to sing.
Like maple seeds,
They travel far and wide,
But they do not escape
For we capture them inside.
When the wind
Converses with the trees,
Those memories talk to you,
And it puts your soul at ease.

Bright Star

Of all the stars
In the heavens above,
You are the brightest
And proclaim our love.
You shine in the sky
And in my heart.
And from neither
Will you ever part.

Endless Time

Now is the time
To care and share
For time will not
Always be there.
It takes but a second
To smile or grin.
That's where many a
Friendship does begin.
Find a few minutes
In every day,
Making it easier
For another's way.
We have lost that chance
With some we did love,
But I'm told time is
Endless with the angels above.

A Gathering

Soft winds blow
Upon my face.
I hasten my step
To keep pace.
You have gone on
Ahead of me,
But there's a time when
All souls will be free.
Will there be a gathering
Of all the clan?
Will it be a place of peace
That we all plan?

Valhalla

On my way to Valhalla,
I met a fräulein.
I stopped for a while,
Drinking fine wine.
We rode white horses
And galloped with the wind,
But when I finally got
There, Odin wouldn't let me in.
He said that my life
Was frivolous at best.
I had to find another
Place if I wanted to rest.

Heavenly Chair

When my time comes,
Save a chair for me.
Welcome me to the gathering,
Glowing faces let me see.
Let me feel the comfort
Of this seat on high.
Sit by me, hold my hand,
Kiss me, and hear me sigh.
I'll not fear
The time has come.
If I'm seated
By someone.
Make it be, my
One true love,
In a heavenly chair
Up above.

Stardust

I've recently heard
The title of a song
And reminded me of a tale
I've known for very long.
When we have passed on and
The world has seen the last of us,
A star somewhere also dies
And becomes stardust.
Each pieces of these stardust
Capture a very small piece of our soul
And carry it forever,
Never again to be whole.
Of the infinite number of
Particles thus created,
Never again will they
Ever be mated.
If, by chance, some
recombining of just a few,
The new life created
Will be called *déjà vu*.
But of the multitude of stardust,
Fragments collecting as life anew,
This combination may exist
With a piece of me or you.

Sails

Sail through the mist
Silently and smooth.
Feel the motion of the waves
And how calm and slowly they move.
You have yet to
Reach the distant shore,
But you know you've traveled far,
And know not how much more
That you have to go before
You have to fold your sail.
But you know there is a
Destination you will reach without fail.

COLLECTION SEVEN

Aging

Clutter

I was shown a picture
Of someone I once knew.
What was her name?
Jane, Mary, or Sue?
When I was young,
I could recall
Mama, dadda, sissa,
Brova—I knew them all.
As we age,
Our world grew.
In our mind, names
Were more than a few.
Envision your mind as an
Attic with clutter.
To get at facts, it's hard
To tell one from the other.
Moving furniture, dust,
And cobwebs for sure.
Getting to people, places,
And things is a chore.
So don't call it
Senility;
It's years of memories to be
Sorted and brought to reality.

Vintage

As if removing a cork
From a bottle of wine,
Savor its aroma,
Then taste that it's fine.
Like emotions that
Pour from you,
Share it with others,
Let them savor it too.
Don't let your life
Stay bottled inside.
Show them your vintage,
Bubbling with pride.

Youth

I can remember when my
Steps were quick and bold,
Not so much now
As I grow old.
A lot of things
Have gone behind,
But they'll always
Exist in my mind.
Look upon what
Was with joy.
Inside of you, there
Is still a boy.
He lightens your load
With a smile and a quip.
Keep him forever
Enjoying your trip.

Don't Fear Life

Fearing life more than death
Means death you have to give.
It requires a strength
To grasp life and live.
When you're being swallowed
By the quicksand of grief,
Remember they're
Always with you, a strong belief.
You will never stand alone,
Feel the support by your side.
Knowing they are always there,
Makes life an easier ride.

Earlier Years

I have weathered through
The spring of my life,
Went through a long summer
With its joy and strife.
Into the fall and
It's almost done.
I hope the winter
Can still be fun.

Peace Within

Sometimes, people care not
What others care or do.
They have grown tired
Of the battles that ensue.
They decide to enjoy
The rest of their years,
Shed confrontation
And allay their fears.
They have found they
Have peace within.
So be happy and content,
Let the new times begin.

Glitter Gone

When the sparkle is
Fading from your eyes
And the glitter is lost
From your golden years, you realize
You're just a few inches
Away from a complete yard.
You can't bring back what's gone,
It's just too hard.
You shake your head,
Thinking of the mistakes you made,
But smile, remembering
All those to whom you gave aid.
Your pages reflect your life
And are far from blank.
Loved ones and friends, both here
And gone, contribute: this, I thank.
When gone, what will
You leave behind?
I believe what will be
Forever exists in your mind.

Decline

As we stand on
The precipice of time,
Each click of the clock
Brings us closer to decline;
But not to fear,
It does not mean the end,
Just another chance
To be united with a friend.
Live in the moment
And hope for a slow pace
Because we're really not ready
To end this race.

Pace of Youth

Many misguided footsteps
Made up our path,
Some caused pain,
Others made us laugh.
It only molded us
Into what we've become.
But we've held onto the
Steps that gave us love from some
And long-lasting friendships
That we hold dear.
Now instead of the pace of youth,
Each step is taken to be slow and clear.

Weigh the Scales

It's said, "Only the good die young."
Maybe that's why I'm still around.
Could it be I'm being kept here
So some good can be found?
Like the scales of justice,
One side weighs good; the other, bad.
I'm sorry I can't change
The life I've had.
I guess, in a way, I should
Be thankful I'm given a chance
To tip the scale in my
Favor and my fortunes enhance.
There's another saying, "Let today be
The first day of your life."
So be the person you can be,
Help others rid their strife.

A Lesser Man

I am but a man,
Plain and simple.
Compared to the universe,
I am less than a pimple.
But once, when I was
A reflection in someone's eyes,
I stood tall in this world.
I could have touched the skies.
Those days have come and
Gone; now my stance is less.
I'm wishing I had them back;
It can't happen, I must confess.

Our Mirror

Like peering into
A looking glass,
Life reflects only
Did we fail or pass.
Was what we did
Worth much at all?
What great triumphs
Can we recall?
Of all the good
Deeds I can muster,
Only one gleams
To a luster.
It was loving you
With all my heart.
Younger we were
When that did start.

Do They Care?

Speak words,
Do they fall on deaf ears?
Tell of all the pleasures you
Visited through the years.
Does anyone really care
Where you've been?
Do they care what you
Did and when?
The importance of your
Meager stay
Has only flourished
In your mind this day.

Rewards

We will walk uphill
And against the wind,
Trudging on life's path
Not seeing an end,
Because we know there
Are rewards that wait.
So we gladly endure
And hasten our gait.
With love, sorrow, and joy,
We have made this trip.
Ahead is unclear,
But more pages will we flip.

The Temple

Why does the
Temple decay
As we attempt to
Make the soul stay?
The essence that
Lies within
Refuses to
Give in.
As the outer
Housing collapses,
We give strength
To our mind to prevent lapses.
I challenge my mind
On a daily basis.
That doesn't imply I
Won't forget dates or faces.

Feeling Age

People say that you are
As old as you feel.
I would like to
Voice a strong appeal.
I certainly am
Not one hundred and three.
Although some days,
It feels so to me.
I have aches in muscles
That I never knew I had.
I look in the mirror
And then feel sad.
Oh, to feel vibrant
And sassy again.
"I'm just a young man,"
I say with a grin and chagrin.

Sands

The sands of time
Accumulate.
They've become a heavy burden
As of this date.
Many years they
Have drifted so.
The memories they have
Stored are yours to know.
If you choose to share
A few grains of sand,
They become part of
Another's sandy land.

Recognition

If ever you meet
Some women or men,
You know you knew them
But know not when.
You ask yourself,
Were they friends or foe?
Is that a smile that
They're trying to show?
They may be as
Confused as you.
So now what is the
Best thing to do?
Well, it makes no
Difference what was past.
Put out your hand,
Be friends at last.

Over the Edge

I have never walked
In the valley of death,
But I have strolled
Along its edges
And have seen others descend
Over the ledges.
I don't know what
They will see when they're there.
I hope they will
Not despair.
I hope all is
Fresh and green,
And they are preparing
A place for us on the scene.

In Twilight Years

If you are in the twilight
Of your years,
Gather up all your might
And belay your fears.
Hold your love,
Let it be fond,
And it will last
You far beyond.

Aging Gracefully

How does one
Age gracefully?
The answer to that
Question is beyond me.
At some point, my step
Lost its bounce.
I've added weight
Ounce by ounce.
Years of gravity
Have caused flesh to sag.
My pace has
Begun to lag.
Luckily, I've
Retained some wit.
I try to share it
With others bit by bit.
My tongue can be sharp,
And won't stay still.
If you do me wrong,
You'll feel that chill.

Under the Skin

Look not at
Their wrinkled skin;
What's important is
Deep within.
Don't dwell on
Their faltering step.
Remember all the
Promises they kept.
Don't think of them
As being old.
Their heart is warm,
And their love not cold.
Don't forget them now or
When they're no longer here.
Tell them you love them now;
When gone, they might not hear.

Always There

Sometimes, as you get older,
There is less room (in your mind)
In your upstairs attic,
So sometimes, things are difficult to find.
Through the years, you try to
Save every bit and piece.
You keep stacking them on
Each other until you can't release
Any people's names, places, or
Things no matter how you try.
It does no good to frown,
Fret, or cry.
The best thing is to don't
Think about them at all.
They will eventually reveal
Themselves come spring, summer, or fall.

Wisps of Air

Sometimes, our thoughts
Are like wisps of air.
You think you feel them,
Then they're no longer there.
No matter how hard you
Try to make them stay,
In a flash of a second,
They are whisked away.
As we grow older, this
Happens more often.
Many dreams and memories
Fly away and are forgotten.

A Name

I was searching for
A name the other day.
Why couldn't I find it?
I know I put it away.
I knew it like the
Back of my hand.
Why couldn't I find it?
I couldn't understand.
Was it Claire, Mary,
Verna, Peg, or Sue?
The harder I tried to find it,
The further away it flew.
There was a time when my
Mind was a keen, sharp blade.
Unfortunately, piling on years
Of information has made it fade.

Child Within

"How are you doing?"
They wanted to know.
As my figure was bent,
And I moved very slow.
Should I lie and
Say, "I'm doing fine."
Or should I admit that
I feel close to dying.
Two persons am I, the one
Outside and other within.
So I gave a chuckle
And sported a grin,
If I could release
The child that I want to be,
You would watch as I
Frolicked, a soul set free.

Blossoms

Blossoms fade,
And petals fall.
But as years go by,
The plant grows tall.
Its beauty shines
And pleases the eye.
It nourishes hummingbirds
And many a butterfly.
Its destiny is,
I don't know why,
To return to dust,
Just wither and die.
But don't weep for
A life well given.
The seeds it spread
Let parts go on living.

COLLECTION EIGHT

Humor

Taller

As you grow older,
I know you grow taller.
Things on the floor
Seem so much smaller,
And when you bend
To pick them up,
They are out of reach
To your touch.
No matter how
You try to bend,
There's no bringing
Your lofty structure to that end.
So you leave it where
It lies
Because you're taller
Than you realize.

Elf

Into the deep woods
I did go,
Looking for some
Company to show.
Then sitting on a
Mushroom, I saw an elf.
Wondering if he was real,
I pinched myself.
"Come, drink from my cup,"
He said with glee.
So I drank some nectar
That he handed me.
After a few more cups
And after a while,
I jumped up on the toadstool
And drank in style.
Then I saw fairies and pixies
Dancing and flitting around.
But all good things must end,
I woke in the morning, lying on the ground.

The Planets

You were my Venus
Here on Earth.
To the rings of Saturn,
You could have given birth.
As big as Jupiter
Was your heart.
Seems by the speed of Mercury,
We were ripped apart.
The oceans of Neptune
I would cross for us.
Will I love you forever?
You bet Uranus.

Piece of Mind

If you ever want to give
Someone a piece of your mind,
Think twice if
You're so inclined.
You may have little
That you can spare.
It may leave a void,
Just be aware.
Sometimes, we think
We know what's best,
But it may be wrong to
Get it off your chest.

Don't Spit

When seas are calm
And your sails are trimmed,
Be content with life
And don't spit into the wind.

Footsteps

I also follow footsteps
In the snow.
Out of curiosity, I want
To know where they go.
I'm the kind of person
Who hates to "miss a trick."
If there's mischief afoot,
I want to be in the thick.
I know of others who
Would join this trail.
Some of them are
No doubt in jail.

Grandfathers

What are
Grandfathers for?
To give big hugs
And ask for more.
To tell the kids to
Put his hand on their heart
And then to pull his finger
(He'll give a big fart).
To tie them down
Cellar to a post. Run upstairs,
Turn off the light, and tell them
The rats like eating kids the most.
Encourage them next time when
They go to school
To ask the librarian if
In the book pool
There is a book
Yellow River by I. P. Daily.
Then he sits back
And grins gayly.
I'm sure other
Grandfathers can add more
Because they understand
What grandfathers are for.

Baseball Game

At times, my life was
Like a baseball game.
Just a *shortstop* to my
Favorite bar I came.
I'd order a large
Pitcher for my thirst.
What could it hurt?
It was only my *first*.
But it tasted so good,
They brought a *second* to me.
Before you knew it, I was
On to the *third* you see.
Then it was to get
Safely *home*
And try to escape
A *hit* on my dome.
In a good mood,
I hoped I would *catcher*.
But as always, I
Would get a stiff lecture.

Bored

Am I really bored,
Do you think?
But I know it takes eight steps to
Get from the table to the sink.
From the sink, it takes twenty-five steps
To get to my reclining chair.
Much restful time
Do I spend there.
When to the bathroom I must go,
Sixty steps there and back.
So far, I haven't got lost;
I've been able to keep track.

What's Real

Did you ever wonder
If your life was real?
Or was it being written
By a monkey with lots of zeal?
Was he thinking he would
Like to live out of the tree
And walk on two legs and
Be completely free?
His story was only full
Of pleasures and joy
When being born, growing up,
And being a little boy.
Little did he know
Of the darkness along the edge,
Fraught with its perils; from
Him, it was hidden knowledge.

A Penny

I stopped to pick up
A penny today.
I couldn't believe some
One would throw money away.
I can remember when ten
Of these meant BBs for my gun.
Many hours plinking cans
And having lots of fun.
Ten would also buy
A Fudgsicle.
What would they buy
Now is hard to tell.

Trouble

Even when I play
Hide and seek,
I swear trouble
Must take a peek
Because it always,
With ease, finds me.
No matter how well I hid,
It pounces with glee,
And even when
I say loudly, "Not it!"
I find myself in
Deep—mud, mire, whatever!

Merriment

I found myself
Dancing on the ceiling
And twirling on the walls;
You snuggled in my arms with feeling.
We moved as one;
Our feet light as air.
Such a special place
With you being there.
It's my dance,
Please don't butt in.
Let me enjoy it
Until I face reality again.

Results

We all play in
The course of time.
I've done so with
Many a rhyme.
Sometimes, it's been
Tongue in cheek.
Other times, when I was
Sad and weak.
A release of emotions
Did I seek.
It's kept me out of
The bars and off the street.

Understanding

There are three ways
To understand a woman.
They are no way impossible
And never because you're a man,
Just as there are three ways
To please her.
That is by saying "you're right,"
"I love you," and "yes, dear."
We are just simple
Minded men,
Believed by women
Every now and then.
This may be true because
We don't like confusion
And realizing wearing the
Pants in a family is just an illusion.

Eggs

People are like eggs; they can
Be soft or hard-boiled or fried to a crisp.
You probably know all these kinds
And many you wouldn't miss.
Also, there are eggheads with
No common sense.
Their minds are scrambled
And not worth two cents.
I like to think mine is
An omelet, blended to the max.
I only have to serve
It up and then relax.

Aghast

Like the reflections
Of a clear, watery pool,
Only glimpses of our lives
Can we reveal.
For to disclose
Our total past
Would leave
People aghast.

Being Serious

Being serious
Can be no fun.
I'd rather be telling
A joke or a pun.
But if you don't
Like my wit,
I really don't
Give a—hoot!

Aw, Coffee

At the brink
Of awakening me
Out of the arms of
Morpheus, I came free.
Cautiously, I slid
From the bed,
Feet on the floor,
Clearing sleep from my head.
As I stood
Coming close to reality,
My choices ahead
Became clear to me:
To shower or
Get coffee first.
I chose not to be clean
But to satisfy my thirst.

Where Was I?

I was writing,
And lost my place,
But I had placed a marker
Just in case.
It would be a shame
If I lost my way.
Then I wouldn't have had
Anything to print today.
Now I offer this
Just to please.
Have a wonderful day
And be at ease.

Forgetfulness

They say that forgetfulness
Comes with age.
Some believe it's
Only a stage.
I believe as you get older,
You've had memories galore
And there is less and less
Room for any more.
So you dust off the cobwebs
And clean up the store
To make room—

Ahhh, I don't remember what
I was going to write next.

The Chips

When all the chips
Have fallen
And the tree's
On the ground,
That's no time to be bawling.
Now you can have
A clear look around.

Heroes

Tom Mix, Gene Autry,
Hoppy, and Roy
Were my heroes when
I was a boy.
They never lost their
White hats throughout any fight.
Their honor was
Their motto and their might.
They always stood for
What was moral and right.
We need more of those
Examples today.
Maybe it would show
Our youth their way.
Just be a friend
Whatever you do.
Can't you still hear Roy
Singing, "Happy Trails" to you?

The Dark Side

Sometimes, we all
Must fight the dark side.
We can use love as the
Light to guide.
We can be torn
Between evil and good.
Dig deep within and
You'll do what you should.
Being true and thoughtful
Is nothing new.
Keep the faith and
"May the force be with you."

Gas

When you look to the sky
While standing by me,
You might be surprised
By what you don't see.
If by the sounds, you
Thought a storm coming,
You'd better look at me,
Grinning and humming.
Don't expect to see
Lightning bolts flying from my ass
When you realize the sound of
Thunder is just me passing gas.

I'll apologize if this little ditty offended anyone; it's just my weird sense of humor.

Odors

Put your face to the ground.
Smell the fresh, clean earth.
Take a walk in the woods.
Open your eyes, get your pleasures worth.
See the majestic trees
And the rocks from ancient times.
Hear the rushing water,
All your senses will combine.
To truly enjoy where we live,
Open your soul and your mind.
Let it set you free
And to nature, be kind.

(Just make sure it's not where
a cow just recently flopped!)

Unnamed Sin

She pursed her lips
And rolled her eyes.
He knew something he did;
She didn't think wise.
He assumed this thing;
She felt an atrocity.
But for the life of him,
He wondered what it could be.
He also knew he should
Just say "I'm sorry, I was wrong"
Than listen to being
Admonished and lectured all week long.
So he bowed his head
And admitted being ashamed
For this terrible sin
That remained unnamed.

A Frog

Kiss a frog
If you will.
Is that what you
Seek as a thrill?
I'm not sure who said
A prince would appear.
They were mistaken;
This, I fear.
I know some men you
Kissed were surely toads,
But as with life,
There are many roads.
I hope you've found that
Someone you kissed
Remains deep in your memory
Even if they're missed.

Zero

Don't you love it when
The temperature drops below zero?
That's when my recliner, with
A blanket, become my hero.
With a hot cup of
Coffee in my hand,
I watch a movie (ocean,
Tropical beach, and sand).
Now I certainly
Don't mind the chill,
But if you have to
Go outside, you will.

COLLECTION NINE

Imagination and Wishes

Imaginative Mind

Walk softly and leave
Momentary footprints in the sand.
Place yourself gently on billowing
Clouds to be taken to a distant land.
Let your dreams be set free,
Sitting next to a glowing campfire.
Climb majestic mountains
And do adventures to which you aspire.
Be with loved ones and friends
Till the end of time.
You can achieve all these
Things with an imaginative mind.

Wishes

How many wishes can
Make up a dream?
There is more to life
Than what it seems.
Who knows what we
Can dream in time?
Or how many mountains
Can we climb?
Create clouds of
Fluffy white.
Make the brightest
Star shine in the night.
Be with the ones
Who you love most.
Be someone of whose
Friendship others can boast.

Nonexistent

Wishes don't exist
In reality.
You would hope
Them to exist in entirety,
But they are like
Fruit left to die
Or plucked by despair,
You would not know why.
If your wishes are
Destined not to come true,
Hold them dear because
They will still exist within you.

Many Years

If you could stop time,
What year would it be?
When sixteen or twenty-five or
Maybe thirty or forty-three?
Think of the most
Precious time of all.
Think of the joy
That your heart can recall.
We can't stop time,
But that's okay
Because all those years
Are in our memories to stay.

Within You

Hold a moonbeam
In your hand.
Fly with your love
To a distant land.
Be tingled by
An ocean breeze.
Climb to towering
Heights with ease.
See a child's smile
And the innocence in their eyes.
All can exist within you;
I know you realize.

A Flame

If you were a flame,
What would you be?
Would you be warm
And toasty or hot and crispy?
Would your dancing and
Flickering soothe the eyes?
Or would your display
Of colors just mesmerize?
Would you bring solace
To the harshness of night?
Would you hold friends
Close within your circle of light?
Would your fiery tongues
Tell if you're strong or weak?
Or would it reflect that the
Love within you is for me to keep?

Hang On

Some wishes we keep
Deep within.
Others we share with
Family and kin.
If by chance
They're granted to us,
Smiles and happiness
Are quite robust.
Others remain
Unfulfilled for a time.
But hang on to hope;
I do with mine.
Keep them alive
For another day.
The most fervent wishes
Will happen if we pray.

Versions

Is there just one version
Of reality?
Is the path the same
for you and me?
Are our hopes and
Desires the same?
Or is it just
A simple mind game?
How I wish I
Could change the past.
How I wish I could
Have made you last.
I am creating a version
If you agree.
We'll be together
For eternity.

Hither Land

I found myself
In a hither land,
Seeing things that
I didn't understand.
Even further out,
The view wasn't so clear.
I tried to focus
To bring it near.
But a veil of mist
Blurred my vision.
It will remain hidden
From me until the veil will risen.

Your Dream

Formidable as
It may seem,
You can conquer
Anything in a dream.
You can talk to a
Butterfly or dragonfly.
You can soar with the
Geese when north they fly.
You can steal a kiss
From the morning dew
And be forever
In the arms of you.

Clear the Reverie

What lurks behind
A reverie?
Sometimes, it is not
Plain to see.
You feel as if you
Should be there
With someone, with
Their love to share.
Focus long enough
To bring it near.
Your true love will
Make it clear.

Wildest Dreams

May your deepest wishes
Reach towering heights
And surpass your wildest dreams
Because what your heart delights
Is within your grasp it seems.

Small Things

See beyond
Your present view.
Imagine what's
In store for you.
Greatness may be
Out of reach,
But could it be a hike up
A mountain or to lay on a beach.
There are many
Things you can do.
Think ahead, make
Them come true.

Memory

You can still wish for
Things you know you can't have.
Then pretend that they're
Granted to you to save.
You have the power within
To make this happen for you,
And in your imagination,
They will be true.
Don't dismiss these flights
Of fantasy so quick
For in your memory,
They will stick.

Whispers in the Shadows

In the evening, I listen to
The whispers from shadows on the wall.
They tell of love and laughter
When we had it all.
I can hear children chattering
As they play from room to room
Or when they're rough-housing
And caused something to go boom.
Tell me the house is settling, and
That's what I hear coming to me.
I know the whispers from the
Shadows are from my true love I can't see.

A Free Spirit

How does one capture a free
Spirit and bring it to paper?
How does one remember just one
Story to describe how great you were?
Where does one start
To begin her tale?
Just like a mist
Settling in a dale,
How do you keep it from
Slipping through your fingers?
Glimpses float freely through your
Mind, but nothing lingers.
Then I find one word I know
That comes close to this task.
That word is love if you
Really had to ask.

Love's Food

Wouldn't it be wonderful
If love grew on trees,
And you could just pick
The amount and kind as you please.
It's a sweetness that would
Increase as it grew,
And you could share
With others whom you knew.
It would bring
Pleasure to your lips
And wouldn't put pounds
On your hips.
You might even can it
For a later date
And bring it forth
To erase some hate.

Fantasy

Flights of fantasy
Fill my head.
Would you have me always
Dealing with reality instead?
What a dreary place on
Earth it would be
If you couldn't create a
World you'd like to see.
These images brought forth
In your subconscious mind
Blossom with love and
Good feelings of all kinds.
They cause you
Not to lose faith
And dream of happiness for
Which you can't wait.

Dream

There was a time that life, like
A gentle stream, flowed by.
Also, a day with the air fresh,
Hardly a cloud in the sky.
My flesh tingled, and
Goose bumps did appear.
My eyes were filled with splender
As my true love drew near.
A touch, a kiss, a hug received
Made it a glorious day.
I only have to dream
To make the memory stay.

Father's Day

A little boy came to me,
And asked, "Mister, why so sad?
It's how my mom looked
When we lost my dad.
Mom said I should write
About all the love he had.
I wrote how I felt when
I was tucked under his arms.
I wrote what fun we had
Visiting the animals on a farm.
I wrote how much I loved him
And was sorry he went away.
I wrote that the missing
Was especially hard on Father's Day.
Mom was right because when
I was done writing this letter,
I felt his love all around me,
And I felt much better."

COLLECTION TEN

Strength

Sometimes

Sometimes, you must
Stand and fight.
Sometimes, you must
Face the night.
Sometimes, you must
Choose what's right.
Sometimes, you must
Feel no fright.
Sometimes, you must
Put enemies to flight.
Sometimes, you must
Show your might.
Sometimes, you must
Hold your love tight.
Sometimes, you must
Let them fade from sight.

Unique

If you ever try to
Walk in another man's shoes
Or if you ever try to
Feel another man's blues,
Just know why you can't
Do such a thing.
Everyone's life story is unique
And their bell a distinct ring.
Seek a way to see within you
And expose the mirror of your mind.
For it's only there within you
That your peace you will find.

Another Look

Anger can project you
To the heights of revenge.
It can satisfy this strong
Emotion again and again.
But as years pass and
You add pages to your book,
What led to that fierce
Anger deserves another look.
Choosing some light reading
And ridding yourself a weighty tome
May bring more happiness to you
And into your home.

Solid Ground

Since the dawn of
Curiosity,
We have looked to
The skies for our destiny.
Then we realized
That here on earth,
Our feet on the ground,
We could find our worth.
Reflecting on things
That we've held dear
Shaped our lives
Through joy and fear.
Living our lives,
Both right and wrong,
Hopefully has made
Us a person who's strong.

Life

Life is full of
Bumps and swerves.
Many things can
Grate on your nerves.
Just when everything
Is great, so you think,
You find out it's not
All rosy and pink.
Just when you're
Dealt blow after blow,
Smile for it must get
Better; this, you know.

A Sturdy Limb

Don't hang your hope
On a willow branch
That is hardly a place
To "bet the ranch."
Find yourself
A sturdy limb.
Grasp it tight.
Get filled with vim.
Let your inner
Spirit flow free.
Hope for good things
For you and me.

Eroding Time

If ever you find
A cliff too steep to climb,
Formidable it seems,
But maybe in time,
you'll conquer its
Heights with ease.
In life as in nature,
You can do as you please.
Problems and cliffs
Are the same, you see.
For time and erosion bring
Them to their knees.

Strength

Stand for what
You believe.
Do not cave in to
Those who try to deceive.
You will succeed, and
You will fail.
But at least
You won't be frail.
You're strength will
Come from within,
And let it carry
You to a win.
A person can only be
As much as his heart desires.
So let your will
Ignite your fires.

Eternal Hope

Eternal hope
Knows no bounds,
And those defeated
Wear no crowns.
Determination is the
Strength of man.
Fulfill your dreams,
Be the best you can.
You need not live
On higher planes.
Make love and kindness
Your image that remains.

COLLECTION ELEVEN

Happiness

Happiness

Happiness is the
Smile of a child,
A kitten purring, or
A day that's mild.
Stand on a mountain
Or lie in clover,
Keep it deep inside,
Your life's not over.
Sing your praises
For what you miss,
A touch, a hug, or
Just a tender kiss.

Start of Day

If you've ever had
Love start your day,
You know that someone
Else was going your way.
Love sometimes comes in
Words spoken quietly
Or with a smile
And a touch made softly.
At times, you just
Know what someone needs
And understand just
How to please;
And when you realize
You're not alone anymore,
Happiness for the rest of
Your life you have in store.

Smile

If you turn your
Smile upside down,
You will only
Produce a frown.
So pucker up
And lick your lips.
Move your feet
And swivel your hips.
Before long,
Joy will appear.
Be with friends
And hold them dear.

Love's Music

To find a place where the music
Of the universe captures your soul,
Think of two people in love,
A disc of gold.
Just listen to this
Melodic refrain
And the vibrations between them.
Then turn up the gain.
There is not a masterpiece
Or a top ten
To soothe you like that
Shared by women and men.

Share

Sprinkle a dash
Of love all around.
Shower it to as many
Friends as can be found.
Rain heavily so the
Love may be returned.
The waters of life are
Filled with what is yearned.

Love

Love is such
A small word,
But finding it
Opens up the world.
Nothing in life
Brings more joy.
It's embodied in the smile
Of a little girl or boy.

Called Love

What is this
Thing called love?
Does it come to you
From up above?
Does it smile on you
Like a clean, fresh dawn?
Does it comfort you
Like cool dew on a lawn?
You can't touch it
Or hold it in your hand,
But it has deep feelings
That you understand.
It comes to you
In many ways.
So hold it close
To warm your days.

A Kitten

The rain fell gently
On her breast,
And I brought her in
At her request.
She snuggled cozily
Into my arm,
Purring softly
Was her charm.
I felt her heartbeat
Close to mine.
She lay contently
For a long, long time.
This kitten, my most treasured
Company of all,
Sharing undying love
As I recall.
I ran my fingers
Tenderly through her hair.
In my memory,
She will always be there.

A Happy Place

Give me
Some space
With the wind
In my face
And the waves
Beating onto the shore.
Let me feel the sand as I walk
And never want for more.
As your senses grow keen
Smelling the salty air.
Your thoughts flow free with
Cooling breezes in your hair.
Your dreams are captured within me;
I'll keep them in a hallowed place.
It's created where I can hold
Your love, and your troubles erase.

To Name a Few

To hear the wind whispering
Or feeling the coolness of dew,
These are some of life's
Pleasures, to name a few.

Seeing a child smile
Or hearing a baby coo,
These are memories to
Cherish, to name a few.

Holding a kitten purring
Or a puppy close to you,
We've all felt these
Pleasures, to name a few.

Looking into the eyes of
Someone who truly loves you,
One of life's greatest
Pleasures, to name a few.

Slivers of Love

Slivers of love
Pierced my skin
And released many
Pleasures from within.
I recall how happy
I was that day.
My only hope was that
They were here to stay.
They filled a void that
I'd had for years.
They comforted my soul
And belayed my fears.

Zipity-Do-Dah

How long has it been since
You've had a zipity-do-dah day?
They come only few times
In one's life come what may.
Was it one of those days
When a miracle came to me?
When two lives became one,
Your soul no longer free.
Or was it when you realized
You cherished a life more than yours?
Or a day when only
The best in life occurs?

A Rush

Life can come at you
Like a rushing train
Or can give you pleasure
Like your favorite refrain.
It can wash over you
Like a falling rain
Or bring forgotten love
To you again.
It can be a panacea
To relieve your pain
Or be your ship of dreams
On the bounding main.

COLLECTION TWELVE

Sounds

Echoes

As I sit and
Talk to the room,
My words echo
Like a sonic boom.
There is no one or
Nothing there to respond,
Only silence as
The words move on.
I have emotions that
I would like to share,
But they drift on the wind,
And go to I know not where.

Free Your Words

Write it down, let
Your words flow free,
Echoed from the tops of mountains
Or felt in the depths of the sea.
Let your emotions speak
What you truly feel.
Don't be afraid for your
Deepest sentiments to reveal.
Feel no shame to cry
Or laugh out loud.
Show to the world
What makes you proud.

Make a Mark

Like a whisper
In the wind,
Another year
Has gone again.
Put your chalk
Upon the slate,
Mark another
Hopeful date.
Fill our dreams,
And fill our glass,
Is that too
Much to ask?

Reverie

I heard a sound
As I sat tonight.
It sounded like
"Are you all right?"
"Looks can be deceiving,"
I replied.
"But I'd be better if
You'd sit by my side."
"Do you know how to
Caress and pet?"
I replied, "It's been a long time,
I tend to forget."
When I close my eyes,
The sound becomes clear.
It's my true love's voice,
Falling on my ear.

Nothingness

Only silence can
Make such a deafening sound.
It weighs heavy
With no one around.
It is a void in
Time and space.
It's nothingness that
Fills no place.
In all the universe
There has to be
At least one sound
Someone will share with me.

Empty Glass

Hear the echoes
From the past.
Let them fill
Your empty glass.
Savor it like
A good wine.
Let it relax you,
Sweetness from the vine.
They will put a rosy blush
Upon your cheek.
It is a pleasure
That we all seek.

Shadows

Heed the shadows
When they speak.
Listen carefully,
They don't repeat.
Sometimes, they speak
Within your mind
For it is there
They are confined,
Telling you of days
Of joy and woe.
Hold them safe,
Don't let them go.

COLLECTION THIRTEEN

Life

Riches

If you were given
A choice in this life,
You could be made a millionaire
Or could have a loving wife.
Would this decision
Be hard to make?
Did you hesitate? If you did,
It was a mistake.
I believe there is
Nothing greater than love.
It is so perfect,
Like a hand in a glove.

Singing

If there comes a time when there's
Not a poem or song in your heart,
Sing anyway even though there
Aren't enough lyrics for the part.
Just know you are living
And your life should go on.
Think of what you had
And carry it beyond.
I will sing your praises
Even out of tune.
I'll sing them in the sunshine
Or under a smiling moon.

Two

If you were asked
To choose one or two?
Would you choose
One or would it be too few?
On the other hand,
You might choose two,
Only to share
Their burdens with you.
A one would make
Your life simple,
But a two might make
You smile with a dimple.
Sitting alone thinking
Of a one or two,
I would certainly choose
Two if it could be with you.

No Wrong Door

When facing three
Doors to choose,
Open one, you win;
The others, you lose.
Is this the way
It has to be?
Do you believe
In destiny?
I believe all the
Doors offer you a trail.
But it's up to you
If you win or fail.
You make the most
Of the hand you're dealt;
Let it be love and
pleasures that you felt.

Come

Come walk with me
As I stroll through life.
Drink with gusto to joy,
Dispense with strife.
Feel the love as
We go along our way.
Hold not your breath,
Let it out to be free.
May only pleasures be
In store for you and me.

Changing Times

Sometimes, I walk to the
Window and just look outside
To make sure there is life
Other than where I reside.
Sometimes, I talk out loud
Just to hear a voice
Or watch a movie,
One of my choice.
There was a time when I
Had friends aplenty.
Now, I'm afraid
Not so many.
Time changes as it
Moves along its way.
Memories seem the
Only things that stay.

Tomorrow

Get up in the morning
And greet the day.
Look life in the eye,
Let it bring what it may.
Say goodbye to the past
With its joy and its sorrow.
Forward is for new friends,
And pleasure's for tomorrow.
Break the mold that is
Holding you down.
Put a smile on your face,
Get rid of that frown.
This is my world,
Put me back on your plate.
Please hold the bus,
I hope I'm not too late.

My Humble Mark

The music of the universe
Is in our souls.
Nature shares its splendors
With the vivid color it unfolds.
I'm in awe of this
Beauty all around.
It has been a time
When pleasures abound.
I know we are but
Specks in the sands of time,
But I try to leave my
Humble mark with a little rhyme.

Face the Day

Each day, when you
Rise from bed,
Are you ready
For what lies ahead?
Do you get up,
Grab it, and growl?
Do you feel like
A tiger on the prowl?
Or are you ready
To retrace your step
And return to
The place you slept?
If the "early bird
Gets the worm,"
Stand your ground
And be firm.

Be Thankful

What is really to understand
About a person's life?
They want love, friends,
And one with less strife.
If they are lucky to
Have any of these,
They can relax
And be at ease.
If these things
Have come and gone,
Be thankful that they
Ever came along.

The Pendulum

The passage of time
Is a precious commodity.
Make each swing of the pendulum
What it ought to be.
We know not what
Each stroke will record.
We hope it's not failure;
We wish for reward.
Like water flowing
Down a hill,
There is no stopping it.
It continues at will.
There is only a certain
Amount given to us all.
So make some history
Be it large or small.

Puzzles

Life is a puzzle
That can't be solved.
Even so, you must
Stay involved.
The intriguing mysteries
It presents with clues
Keep us challenged
So we can't refuse.
It teases even
The faint of heart,
And the bold say,
"Where do we start?"

A Blank Page

Walk softly and leave
Gentle prints on the ground.
Hope that you'll have
Had love all around.
There's a blank page to be
Written on when you've gone.
Will it be pleasant reading
Like loving words of a song?
Maybe it will bear
Harsh words by some, I fear.
Let's cast out those of anger
And hold the ones of love forever near.

Bygones

Perhaps, the day
Will come
When there will
Be peace for some.
They will quell
Their troubled minds
And leave their
Wounds far behind.
I hope that day
Will come for me
And let my
Bygones be history.

Material Things

Material things are the most
Important to some.
Don't they realize
You don't get love and caring from
The possessions you can touch.
It's only the feelings
Within that really mean so much.
You can't take much with you
When you leave,
Only the intangibles
And what you believe.
So cherish what's in your heart.
Share yourself,
It's the best part.

A Perfect Time

I don't know of
A perfect time
When all was right
With no decline.
But there were times
High on our list
When we recall
With no remiss.
Our love was special,
But only our family knew
That our lives were
Where love grew.

You Are Your Guru

Why seek a guru
To tell you right from wrong?
It's been inside
You all along.
You may have chosen
Badly along the way,
But no need for it
To be an anchor to stay.
Rid yourself of wrongs
That may have been.
Seek out more
Forgiving men.
Nothing you say or do
Will change the past.
Let those without
Wrongs the first stone cast.

Greatest Place

I've been in places
On this earth,
And I'll tell you,
For what it's worth,
No matter if you've gone
Long distances forth,
There is only
One absolute truth.
When you return,
This is no mirth,
Home is the
Greatest place on earth.

Bitterness

If you let bitterness
Fill your cup,
It will eventually
Eat you up.
It's over and done,
For what it's worth,
So bury it in
Tons of earth.
Let it go
Into the past
And be at peace with
Yourself at last.

Some Place

Somewhere,
There exists
A place where
You'll be missed.
It may be in
Someone's mind
Or in another
Place undefined.
But if there is
Just one,
You can really say
That you've won.

A Woman's Love

A woman's love can
Be as deep as the ocean.
All it requires from a man
Is his trust and devotion.
She can create calm seas
Or storms with her emotion.
White caps and waves
Are her love potion.
Your heart is captured
With her tidal motion,
And your love is rewarded
With her soothing salty lotion.

What Life Is About

"Take my hand
And walk with me
For there is much in
This world for you to see,"
The father said to
His child of three.
As they strode along,
She asked of he,
"How did such
Beauty come to be?"
"It was painted by
A hand so free
That the when and
Why are a mystery.
Don't ever close your
Eyes and shut it out.
This is what life
Is all about."

Own My Heart

Struggling with life,
I lost my way.
Somehow, she found me
And brought me back that day.
She dug deep into my soul
And ferreted out
That voice within me
That wanted to shout,
"Is there love out there
Or am I all alone?"
She gave me that love,
And my heart she did own.
Many years of comfort and
Love did we share.
A rescued soul and an
Angel became a pair.

Your Time

A time to imagine,
A time to ponder,
A time to dream
And let your mind wander.
A time to cry
Over times that were fonder.
A time to rejoice
And be filled with wonder.
A time to smile
And let your heart recover.
A time to hope for
Calm waters up yonder.

COLLECTION FOURTEEN

Memories

Cherishing

As you go forth
To greet the day,
Remember those you've
Lost along the way.
Remember a smile,
A touch, or a kiss.
What's the best about
Them that you miss?
Fill your glass
And drink a toast.
Hang on to the memory
You cherish the most.

Only for You

There are flowers that
Bloom only for you.
There are thoughts that
Bring peace only for you.
There was one true
Love only for you.
There are memories of
Life only for you.
Until the curtains
Close around you,
These pleasures will
Have to do.

Inner You

When you're sad
And feeling blue,
Just take a minute
To reach your inner you,
For it is there
Where memories reside.
The times where
Love was bona fide.
Bring it forth,
Cherish the smile,
And be at peace
For a long, long while.

Fortunate

I capture a glimpse
Of a faded memory.
I enjoy how it stirs
Emotions within me.
I know they're gone, and
I can't bring them back,
But I have a feeling of love for
Which there is no lack.
I carry it with me
For the rest of my days.
I am fortunate for
These momentary displays.

A Cup

If your cup is empty
And you stand alone,
Fill it up with
Memories that you own.
With a soothing sight
Of long ago,
Absorb all the essence
You can know.
Now your cup is full,
And you can stand fast.
Believe what lies ahead
Is a reflection of your past,
And the love you had
Will be back with you at last.

COLLECTION FIFTEEN

Help

Needs

Keep a candle burning
For those in need.
When I needed help,
It was gladly received.
A hand up or a
Pat on the back,
Try to share what
Others may lack.
A loving touch or
A simple smile
May be all they need
To keep going for a while.

Not the Whole

Pity the people who
Are so full of themselves
That there is no
Room to accept love, joy, or elves.
There is merriment, quip,
And twinkle of the eye.
Look beyond why you
Think you're so great.
Many pleasures can be
Had if you would just relate.
See the world and what
It has in store for your soul.
Realize you are but a
Part, not the whole.

Silent Night

There are cheerful days
And silent nights.
See everyone smile
At the season's sights.
But don't forget
To do all you can
For those in need and
The downtrodden man.
This is a season of giving,
Have a ball.
The best gift is love.
Bless you all.

No Bias

It is the
Air that we breathe,
It is each
Day we believe
That we have done
Some good to others,
That we have friends
We call brothers.
No bias dwelt
Where it didn't belong,
Only toward others
Who had done us wrong.
Our visions simply go
To the soul
For it is only within
Where lies our whole.

Giving Back

Don't turn your
Back on fellow man.
Give them all the
Help you can.
Life has a way
Of giving back,
So for kindness,
Don't you lack.
But there are
Things one can't forgive.
With these ill feelings,
You will have to live.

COLLECTION SIXTEEN

Paths

A Toast

As we bid goodbye
To a challenging year,
Lift your glass and
Toast those you hold dear.
We must say bon voyage
To ones we've lost,
Losing them was
A terrible cost.
But drink heartily with
Those still by your side
And hope next year is
One hell of a ride.

Paths

We have had many paths
Offered to us every day.
How we choose isn't
Our total way.
Don't regret that at
One was a fail.
There are still others
To put wind in your sail.
Your path is not
Straight and narrow.
It winds through your life,
Offering a great tomorrow.

A Shaft of Light

Into the darkness,
A shaft of light flew.
It was given for many
But only accepted by few.
It promised to lead
You on a safe path,
Bring joy to your life.
Midst people who laugh,
Have no fear.
Walk into the light.
Believe in the journey
With all your might.

A Plan

Due to circumstances,
We've been given time to reflect.
Step back and analyse
What has been our trek.
Are we happy with
Our current path?
Or should we plot another
Direction on our life's graph?
Look closely at what you
Might like to change
And lay out a plan.
Is it in range?
What do you need to
Do to bring it into view?
Seek any way to achieve,
Set your sights to renew.
If you decide it's worth doing
When all is said and done,
Rise with the sun tomorrow.
It's a new day you've just begun.

The Candle

I've lit a candle in case
You've lost your way.
It may brighten your path
And ease your burden today.
At times, we all
Need a fiery glow
To bring us back
To the comfort we know.
Life is complicated
And keeps you in the dark
When all that is
Needed is a little spark.

Safe Path

A shaft
Of light
In the darkness
Of night
Helps to
Light your way
So safely on
The path you'll stay.
Very easy
It is to stray.
Love will
Keep harm at bay.

COLLECTION SEVENTEEN

Future

Ahead

In my mind, I stood,
Looking down the way.
What lay ahead
Was so foggy, I couldn't say.
Would I really want
To clear the mist
To know if by
Destiny, I'd be kissed?
Knowing what the
Future brings
Would only remove
The hope of things.
Living each day
And wanting the best
Put a lid on
All the rest.

Nagging Mysteries

I am haunted by
What I don't know
And by what the
Future might show.
The nagging mysteries
Hidden in the mist,
I can never see clearly.
It's as if clenched in a tight fist.
I try to peer deeply
Into the unknown.
It is naught because
It is not mine to own.

What Will Be

In the stillness
We contemplate
Things that have
Happened as of this date.
We also weigh the
Present against the past,
Thinking of things
That could have last.
The future we
Cannot see.
Does it hold a mystery
That will be kind to me?

Celebrate

I raise my glass
And toast you all.
Whether you celebrate
Quietly or have a ball,
Take a moment to reflect on
What's gone by.
Then welcome the future,
Let your aspirations fly.
Who knows what
Great things await;
I'll cross my fingers
And mark this date.

COLLECTION EIGHTEEN

Friends

Friendships

A fortune lies
Within your grasp,
All you have to
Do is ask.
It's called friendship,
But they aren't cheap.
Treat them with honor
And they'll be yours to keep.
They are one of the most
Precious gems of all.
Be true to them and
You can stand tall.

Pages of My Mind

At least half as many
People now share my life.
I've lost many good
Friends—even my wife.
It is said that they
Go to a better place
When they leave
The human race.
Their journeys have been
Written on the pages of my mind.
They make me smile and laugh with
All the times they were kind.
So they will truly never be
Gone from my heart
Even though we are
A kazillion miles apart.

True Friends

Friends is a precious word
For it means they do
Not come in second or third.
They offer you a shoulder
When in need.
For they are not
A dying breed.

Close Friends

Many close friends have come
And gone throughout my life,
Passed to oblivion but
Not forgotten—even my wife.
Now I count them on
One hand, few are their files.
Those still here are
Separated by many miles.
But remembering the fun
We had brings nothing but smiles.
Making new friends as
Close and trusting is an impossible task.
To find just one more in
My lifetime, is it too much to ask?
The memories of what we
Had is all I have to keep.
These are alive in
My dreams when I sleep.

Shed a Tear

We've stood beside
Some valued friends.
Some are cherished memories
When their lives end.
Their number has
Become less each year.
Thinking back on them,
We shed a tear.
But now we search
High and wide
To find another valued
Friend to stand beside.

Defy Time

True loves and good friends
Weather the test of time.
Whether they're near or far,
They always have a space in your mind.
Ages upon ages they will
Always exist.
True loves and friends
Will always be missed.

Trusted Friends

How many people
Would you really trust?
Who would stand by you
Be they alive or dust?
True friends are
Hard to find.
Those having your back
Are a special kind.
I'm happy to say
I've had a few
And thankful for
The ones I knew.

Sing Me a Song

Sing me a song
Of love tonight.
Make me feel that
All is all right.
Let my dreams
Wash my worries away
So I can wake tomorrow
To a bright, fresh day,
Facing the future
As half a man.
I'll overcome tomorrow
As best I can.

By Your Side

If you would like,
I'll stand by your side.
But if you prefer, I'll
Go; this, you can decide.
I'll be a good friend
Through thick and thin.
Just say the word and
Our friendship will begin.
You never have to worry
If I'll protect your back.
An infinite amount of caring
And it will not slack.
So smile and give
Your hand as a welcome sign.
This will be written on
Life's pages: yours and mine.

Stories

I've poured you a glass,
Come sit a spell.
You have many stories
That I want you to tell.
I know they will
Be both happy and sad,
Remembering the long life
That you've had.
Tell of the love
That caused you to soar.
I'll refill your glass if
You'll keep telling more.

About the Author

His emotions varied from day-to-day, as evidenced by what is written. He has bared a large part of his life.